high vibrational *think*

G000141165

how to
feel great
about
yourself

steve wharton

foulsham

LONDON • NEW YORK • TORONTO • SYDNEY

foulsham

The Publishing House, Bennetts Close, Cippenham,
Slough, Berkshire, SL1 5AP, England

ISBN 0-572-03076-2

Copyright © 2005 Steve Wharton

Cover photograph © Powerstock

A CIP record for this book is available from the British Library

Printed in Great Britain by Cox & Wyman Ltd, Reading, Berkshire

Contents

Dedicated to my children, James and Amy.

I love you very much.

You Can Feel Great About Yourself!

Feeling good about yourself changes your whole life – but how can you achieve it? A vast number of books have been written on the subject of feeling good, achieving success and realising your dreams, offering solutions packaged in every possible format. Many of these books offer fascinating ideas, suggest answers to profound philosophical questions and delve deep into the mysteries of the subconscious mind. Some of them have, indeed, succeeded in making life better for some people some of the time.

But is there a simpler answer to the question, 'Can I feel really good about myself?' I believe that the answer is yes. In fact, I will be much bolder than that – I *know* that the answer is yes.

Religion, philosophy, psychology and science all have their part to play in helping us to learn more about ourselves and how we interact with one another, but for ordinary people they can sometimes be just too confusing. And for many people – even when they have gained a huge amount of knowledge from studying these disciplines – something is still missing from the equation. It's a bit like offering good advice on how to drive a car but forgetting to mention that you need a key to turn the engine on.

It is my belief that high-vibrational thinking – or HVT – offers that key. Like a key, it is neat, it is simple, and it unlocks a whole new understanding of how the world works. The simplicity of HVT is undeniable, making it accessible to anyone and everyone from all walks of life. You don't need a degree in rocket science – or anything else – to grasp the principals of HVT. In fact, I have yet to meet anyone who didn't immediately understand it and see how they could put it into practice – and I have run courses for children as young as ten years old.

HVT offers a way of looking at the world and how we work together from a simple, new perspective. The concept can be applied to any aspect of your life, but here we are going to look at the fundamentals: how to feel good about yourself, whoever you are and whatever you have achieved – or not achieved – in your life so far.

Once you understand the principles, you can begin to implement my six-week programme, which will empower you to change your life for the better. It will help you really to like yourself, to extend and realise your potential and to begin to achieve the things you want in life. Problems that may before have seemed insurmountable will be cut down to size. Goals that may have seemed way beyond your reach will no longer seem outside your grasp.

To understand how incredibly empowering HVT can be, we first need to break it down to the nuts and bolts. This will give you a clear and concise picture of its fundamental principles so that you can use it effectively.

Our World of Energy

'If you want to find the secrets of the universe, think in terms of energy, frequency and vibration.' Dr Nikola Tesla, 1942

Dr Nikola Tesla was one of the foremost scientists of the early twentieth century. His outstanding intellect paved the way for a large number of modern technological developments; in fact the tesla coil is still used in many television sets today. It is amazing to think that his words in 1942 should be still so relevant today. We now know that his understanding of the universe as energy, frequency and vibration was quite accurate. As we explore the intricate workings of the universe, unlocking the secrets of this amazing world of energy in which we live, this fact only becomes clearer.

Nothing you see around you is quite as it seems! The world that we live in is a huge ocean of energy, taking many different forms. The age of the microscope has shown us abundantly clearly that things that appear solid and static to us are in fact nothing of the sort. Even if the only science you know has been learnt from TV dramas about forensic scientists, you will be aware that if you look at an apparently solid object at a sufficiently powerful magnification, you will find that it is made up not of a single solid substance but of tiny particles vibrating at phenomenal speed. These tiny particles are known as neutrons, electrons and protons, and they link together to form atoms, the most basic building blocks of life.

What is perhaps even more astonishing is that atoms actually consist of 90 per cent empty space, which – by logical deduction – means that what we think of as solid, such as a concrete wall, is in fact mostly not solid at all! Nothing around us is actually solid, even though it may appear so; everything is made up of energy, vibrating constantly and at various frequencies. This applies to everything you see around you: trees, houses, cars, walls, roads, dogs, cats, fish. It is a fundamental law of physics and applies even to us humans.

Each of these millions upon millions of different forms of energy vibrates at a specific frequency. The frequency at which it vibrates influences the form of the object. For example, the molecules of a solid vibrate very slowly; the molecules of a liquid vibrate more quickly; and the molecules of a gas vibrate even more quickly. Thus something with the same chemical composition can take different forms depending on the vibrational frequency of its molecules. When the molecules are vibrating at a medium frequency rate, water appears as a liquid. Slow down that frequency and you get ice; speed up the frequency and you get steam.

We are all part of the vibrant ocean of energy
As I have said, we are just as much a part of this cycle of energy as everything else around us. High-vibrational thinking is based on that fact. Its fundamental principal is that we need to learn to see and think about our world in terms of energy.

High-vibrational thinking is a revolutionary new concept that teaches us how to have some control over the incredible universe of energy that we live in. It offers a way of seeing people – and the interactions between people – as part of a unique energy transmission process that is hugely empowering to the individual. The first part of this book explains exactly how the system works. If you go back to fundamentals, it is really very easy to understand.

Just as ice, water and steam vibrate at different frequencies, so emotional energy also vibrates at different frequencies. As I will be explaining in detail later, positive emotions are high-vibrational energies, while negative emotions are low-vibrational energies. If we can find a way to maintain high-vibrational energy and deflect low-vibrational energy, then we can change our whole perspective on life. That's what HVT can help us to do. HVT is a system that takes positive thinking into an exciting new dimension.

HVT changes your perspective

This realisation throws a whole new light on how we perceive our world. Indeed, knowing how to use this information – and I'll be showing you that too – can be hugely liberating and empowering, because it offers a way of using our knowledge to handle our lives in a more beneficial and productive way. This new perspective gives you far greater control over everyday situations and events that you may previously have thought were largely beyond your control. With this knowledge comes power, and that power is the ability to choose more carefully how you relate to the energies that affect your life.

HVT will become automatic

What's more, once you have learnt how to use this power, it will become an automatic way of thinking, and you can gain the benefits without even having to make a conscious choice about it. Once you have learnt to walk, you don't need to think consciously about the process any more. It's the same with HVT. Once you understand HVT, you will

you automatically begin to incorporate it into
 ᴜʀe as a working practice without any conscious
effort on your part. Its positive influence on your life will
be automatic, as the truth of HVT, once learnt, cannot be
ignored. Using HVT on a daily basis becomes a natural
habit that will benefit every aspect of your life and help
you to change in a positive and fulfilling way. All of a
sudden, you will find that something inside you is
monitoring the events and situations in your life and
automatically responding to negative situations in a way
that will prevent them from dragging down the frequency
of your energy field and making you feel bad.

A paradigm shift in consciousness occurs when you use
HVT. You find yourself able to deal with the negative events
and situations that are part of everyday life in a new and
positive way. HVT enables you to take control of events
and situations rather than allowing them to control you.
This is incredibly liberating, freeing your mind to direct
your life in a much more productive and focused way.

Let's look at a simple example from an HVT course I
recently ran. Within days of attending the course, two of
my students found themselves turning off a particular
television programme that they had been watching
regularly for many years. They did not think about this
action consciously until weeks later when it came up in
conversation. Another student was talking about how
negative this television programme had become. At that
point, they both realised they had made the decision not to
watch it any more immediately after attending the HVT
course. Subconsciously they had sensed its negative impact
and put a stop to it.

This kind of reaction is common among people who
attend HVT courses, because they quickly learn to avoid
engaging with damaging negative energies. You are already
starting to learn that lesson simply by reading this book.

You too can learn automatically to handle situations and decisions in a more positive and beneficial way.

Essentially simple

The real strength of HVT is its simplicity and the fact that when applied to any subject it breaks it down to a few basics. This enables anybody, whatever their age or background, to gain an understanding that previously may have seemed impossible. This is one of the reasons we have had so much success in working with children as young as ten years old. Young people absorb the concept very quickly and find it easy to think in terms of HVT about every area of their life.

It also means that the technique can be applied to any aspect of your life, regardless of your occupation or lifestyle. At school, it can give your more confidence and enthusiasm and help you to perform well. At work, it can cut out negativity, create a better atmosphere and even increase productivity. In the home, it can reduce arguments and create a more loving environment.

Essentially, HVT is about making you feel good about yourself and maintaining that feel-good factor whatever life throws at you. Just think how much happier that could make you – not to mention the immeasurable stride forwards in terms of moving our world into a brighter, high-vibrational future.

How Emotional Energy Vibrates

Now we understand that the whole world is part of a complex energy system, let's look specifically at how that affects us. Here, we are talking in terms of the power of emotional energy, and that is what we can harness to work to our advantage with HVT.

We have seen that – just like the objects around us – we are made up of energy and – like all forms of energy – our personal energy field vibrates constantly. The vibrational frequency of our energy field is affected by our thoughts and feelings. These are also made up of energy waves, and they influence our lives much more profoundly than we may realise. So depending on how we are feeling at any given time, the frequency at which our energy field vibrates can change dramatically.

Scientists and researchers in the USA have measured the frequency of the energy waves transmitted by the emotion of love, which they found vibrate very quickly, or at a very high frequency. Similarly, they measured the frequency of the energy waves transmitted by the emotion of fear, which they found vibrate very slowly, or at a low frequency. Our world exists within these two parameters.

Love is transmitted on a short wavelength, so it has a fast, high-vibrational frequency.

Fear is transmitted on a long wavelength, so it has a slow, low-vibrational frequency.

Think for a moment about listening to the radio, and this will help you to understand how energy waves work. Radio stations are constantly transmitting radio waves. These are in the air all around us, even though we cannot actually see them. If your radio is not tuned in to the right frequency, all you will hear is an annoying hiss. However, if you tune in your radio to the right frequency, you will be able to pick up on those radio waves so that you can hear and understand them perfectly, whether they are transmitting music, news, drama or comedy.

Happy is a high vibration
So whatever we are thinking and feeling has a very real effect, as it alters the frequency of our personal energy field. If we are happy, our energy is high-vibrational; if we are sad, our energy is low-vibrational. I am sure you are already getting the idea. Similarly, we can be affected by other people's thoughts and feelings. If you are unlucky enough to be in a room full of bored or unhappy people, it is very hard to remain upbeat and cheerful.

When we are full of laughter and joy, it makes us feel good. What is actually happening is that the high-vibrational energy of joy has pushed up the frequency of our personal energy field. We also experience this effect when we achieve something good, such as passing a driving test or an exam, scoring a goal, winning a competition, or receiving praise for a job well done. What is happening here is the same: the achievement has made us feel suddenly successful and good about ourselves, again pushing up the frequency of our personal energy field.

So, as you can see, any thoughts and feelings that are positive – laughter, joy, honesty, sincerity, truth, compassion – are high-vibrational, keeping our energy field vibrating at the higher levels and therefore making us feel good. Just think about some of the expressions we use to describe that kind of feeling: 'I'm high as a kite', 'I'm buzzing', 'My mind's racing'. They are referring to the frequency of our personal energy field, and they clearly demonstrate that wonderful elation. The faster our energy field vibrates, the better we feel, because that means we are closer to the frequency of love.

Of course, the opposite is also true. Anger, frustration, hate, jealousy, envy, greed and selfishness are all negative thoughts and feelings. Such emotions are low-vibrational; they slow down our energy field and make us feel bad. This is why we use phrases such as 'I'm down in the dumps' or 'I'm flat as a pancake'. The lower our energy field vibrates, the closer we are to the vibration of fear – which is not where we want to be!

Increasing our vibrational frequency

Even though this may be the first time you have thought about it in these terms, you will probably recognise that we spend most of our time trying to feel good about ourselves. In HVT terms, that means we are constantly seeking to increase our vibrational energy frequency.

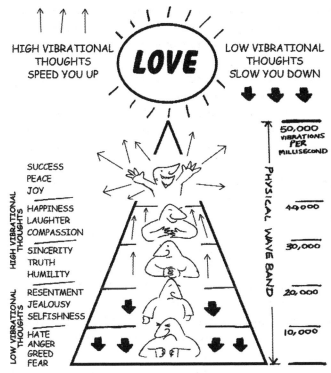

Hypothetically speaking, the physical waveband may run from 0 to 50,000 vibrations per millisecond. Our energy fields fluctuate between these parameters in our day-to-day lives. When we are happy and enjoying life, we may be vibrating at 35,000 vibrations per millisecond, but this may fall to 6,000 vibrations per millisecond when we are down in the dumps.

There are any number of ways to try to do this – getting your hair done, buying new clothes, having a drink, going to the gym, planning a special night out. They can all be effective, but if they don't alter your fundamental emotional state, the effect is not going to last very long. If you have ever got a buzz from buying a new pair of shoes, only to feel low again by the time you got home because you had nowhere to go to show them off, you'll know what I mean.

Some people take the search for a high to extremes, experimenting with drink and drugs. This may give a temporary 'high' but can very soon have the serious negative result of addiction.

That's where HVT comes in, because it is a way of educating ourselves so that our normal vibrational frequency is higher – plus it teaches us to control the effects of low-vibrational energy from other sources. It's just like exercising regularly to increase your resting heart rate. This not only makes you feel fitter but it also makes it easier for you to cope with the physical demands of your everyday life.

How Our Emotional Frequency Is Established

As we spend most of our time trying to raise our vibrational frequency in order to feel better about ourselves, it makes sense to have a look at the factors that determine our individual energy level in the first place. This energy level is established and controlled primarily by our subconscious mind.

The conscious and subconscious mind
Your conscious mind is what you use to go about your everyday life – paying the bills, cleaning, sorting the washing, going to work. This is the methodical, reasoning part of your mind that carries out the daily tasks. It is the organised, sensible, logical part of you that understands how your world works. Your conscious mind automatically analyses any situation it confronts and plots the best and most logical way to deal with it.

Your subconscious mind, on the other hand, is a more complex entity, and is a source of immense power. It is affected by your surroundings in much more subtle ways and reacts most strongly to emotional stimuli.

Many psychologists refer to the subconscious mind as the 'inner child', because they feel that this best describes its characteristics. This terminology can help us to understand why our subconscious can sometimes pull us towards something that is not good for us. Imagine yourself as a child of five years old, with all the feelings and wonderment you had at that age; now imagine that this child is real and living inside you. Now you have a picture of your subconscious mind. It does not reflect you as you are now, with everything you have experienced and learnt over the course of a lifetime, but you as you were then. This child has no concept of what is good or bad for

Your inner child (your subconscious mind) will do everything it can to keep you in your comfort zone, even if this means holding you back in your life.

you; it just has its programming, which it will try to stick to regardless of what you may or may not consciously want.

In other words, we are all going through life trying to make some kind of progress but subject to the limitations that our subconscious mind places upon us. In terms of energy, our subconscious monitors us on a daily basis to keep us in what it has defined as our normal vibrational frequency zone.

Our formative years

The most important factor in determining this normal or average vibrational frequency level is the first five or six years of our lives. It is during these formative years that we establish our general thought patterns about ourselves. These first five or six years effectively programme our subconscious mind with certain beliefs about ourselves, which we then carry throughout the rest of our lives and which are very difficult to change. This vibrational frequency programming sets the boundaries for us and has a major bearing on every aspect of our life from then on.

The most influential factors in our development are our immediate family and the environment we grow up in. In other words, the vibrational frequency of our environment and the frequency level of our family are what we pick up and become used to as our norm. When our mind is young and impressionable during those early years, we readily accept the situation in which we find ourselves. Because we don't know of any other situation, we unquestioningly believe that this is where we belong. This becomes the frequency zone we feel comfortable in and which, subconsciously, we spend virtually the rest of our lives trying to stay in.

So if you were brought up in a family with not much love (high-vibrational energy), you will believe that you only deserve a certain amount of love in your life, and your subconscious will use all its power to make sure that that is what happens. This will have massive repercussions, affecting your relationships, your work – in fact, everything you do in life. Your subconscious will stick to the programming, whether it's good for you or bad for you. In other words, it will monitor your vibrational frequency and keep it at the level that it is programmed to do.

As we grow up, our subconscious beliefs tend to become self-confirming because we constantly play them over in our subconscious mind, reaffirming our opinions and thoughts about ourselves. Most of the time, we are completely unaware that we are doing this. When we are constantly affirming to ourselves that we are not worthy (worthy meaning deserving of love, the highest-vibrational energy), we are keeping our vibrational frequency at the lower levels – and making life much harder for ourselves. The opposite is also true. If we constantly circulate high-vibrational thoughts about ourselves, we will keep our vibrational frequency at the higher levels, which in turn affirms that we are worthy and makes our life run much more smoothly.

Your inner child (subconscious mind) is much more in control of your life than you realise.

Of course, we have to acknowledge that we are all different and unique individuals with many varying factors determining our personality. This is why different people emerge from a similar upbringing with a different attitude to life. However, you are almost certainly reading this book because at least one aspect of your life can be improved, and understanding where any negative input may have come from is the first step towards being able to change the negative and maximise the positive.

The comfort zone

The energy level that we feel is where we belong is often referred to as our 'comfort zone'. We find it very difficult to break out of this zone, as our subconscious mind constantly draws us back to it as its starting point, regardless of whether it is in fact good for us or bad for us. This may seem strange but is in fact quite logical.

We tend to mix and feel more comfortable with people of a similar vibration rate.

You may, for example, feel uncomfortable in an upmarket, expensive restaurant, or perhaps you feel nervous when talking to professional people such as lawyers or consultants. What you are experiencing is a reaction to the frequency of the environment or person – if the frequency is vibrating at a higher rate than yours, you will probably feel slightly uncomfortable. This means you will seek out places and people with which you share a similar frequency, as this is where you naturally feel most comfortable.

Imagine carrying around with you an identity card that has not only all your personal details but also all your unconscious beliefs about yourself printed on it. If your normal vibrational frequency is low, your ID might list some of the following:

- ▸ You will only be shown a limited amount of affection from people who are close to you
- ▸ You are only allowed to have a low-paid job
- ▸ You are only allowed to live in a small house
- ▸ You are only allowed to have an old car
- ▸ You are only allowed to be average in what you do
- ▸ You are only allowed to wear casual clothes
- ▸ You will only be able to achieve a limited amount of success
- ▸ You will only ever have difficult relationships
- ▸ You will only ever have friends who take advantage of you

Now imagine that if you try to step out of line by going against these guidelines, you will be confronted by a police officer whose job it is to keep you within their confines. Let's say you manage to get a good job that pays well. Before you know it, the officer is on your case and starts talking you out of the job. You may find that you can't motivate yourself to raise your level of achievement as you need to in order to do the job well, so you start to make excuses and lay the blame elsewhere. Instead, you tell yourself that you work too hard or the firm is taking advantage of you, the pay is not adequate or you are not appreciated. This undermines your confidence and your ability to do the job well, and before very long you will find a way to give up the job while blaming everyone else.

I have seen this happen in my own experience. A very capable employee suddenly, after about three months in the job, begins to under perform. They start coming in late with any old feeble excuse, they cultivate an attitude of not been appreciated, they disrupt the other staff and in the end they push you so far that you have no choice but to let them go. When this happens, they insist that they are being victimised, they have done nothing wrong, and they may even threaten to take you to a tribunal. What they fail to acknowledge – even to themselves – is that it is their own behaviour that has caused the problem. The police officer has done his job and dragged them back into their low-vibrational comfort zone.

The problem with this situation is that we don't realise what is happening – that it is our own subconscious mind that is wreaking such havoc in our lives. It does not seem logical to believe that we would sabotage our own efforts, so we assume that the fault lies elsewhere.

I have experienced this myself, so I know how easily it can occur. When I was at school I was quite good at sport and soon found myself playing for the school teams. I did very well, and at one point it was expected that I might go on to a higher level. Once I realised that this was in prospect, I couldn't seem to motivate myself any more and decided to stop playing altogether. At the time, I just decided that I didn't feel like playing any more; it was only years later that I realised what had taken place. The threat of success had triggered off my subconscious programming, which dictated that I didn't deserve the high-frequency feelings that success could bring. These would have pushed me out of my comfort zone and into a new higher-frequency zone, so my subconscious mind convinced me that I didn't like sports any more and made me feel tired and unmotivated when faced with a game. Unfortunately for me, my subconscious won, and at 14 years of age I hung up my boots and as a result missed many years of enjoyment.

Not better but different

One thing always to remember, however, is that even if you start out with a low-vibrational energy field and feel uncomfortable with a different group of people, they are not 'better' than you. We all have our own qualities, strengths and weaknesses. You may want to be more like someone who has a high-vibrational energy field because they are fun to be around and are positive and more successful – that's fine. But that doesn't make them intrinsically better than you. Envy and self-criticism are both low-vibrational emotions, and if you give way to them, it will only make things worse.

You may, on the other hand, be someone who has had a good upbringing in a high-vibrational environment, leaving you with high-vibrational thought patterns. This gives you a much better chance of making the most of your life and better equips you to take advantage of opportunities that arise. You may still feel uncomfortable in places or with people where the energy pattern does not match your own – probably because your personal energy field is vibrating at a higher frequency – but it is important that you do not fall into the trap of believing that this makes you better in some way, for this is a damaging thought pattern. Arrogance and self-importance will pull down your energy frequency.

Don't try to place blame

It is important to point out here that your parents and their parents before them were also subject to this subconscious programming. However they brought you up, they were doing their best within their own programmed mental confines.

It is essential that you do not try to attach blame to anybody for your life as it stands at the moment. This would be to go straight down the low-vibrational route. Such thought processes are negative and low-frequency; they are certain to act as a dead weight around your neck and pull you down. Pointing the finger at others serves no purpose and will only harm you – by lowering your vibrational frequency. This is the time to assess the past and move on to the new, high-vibrational you.

How Our Emotional Frequency Affects Our Lives

The easiest way to demonstrate how limiting it can be to allow your subconscious mind to remain in control of your life is to take a look at a few examples.

Paul's comfort zone with crime

A few years ago, my work brought me into contact with a sales representative who proceeded to tell me a bit about himself. Let's call him Paul. Paul was brought up in a fairly tough environment, and his father had not been around much, as he had spent most of his time in prison for relatively minor offences. However, this childhood grounding had taken its toll, and, at 12 years old, Paul had found himself in trouble with the police for the first time for a minor crime. His family considered crime as a profession and accepted it as a normal way of life so, far from chastising him for having committed a crime, they were more concerned that he had not got away with it. This pathway continued. Paul's teenage years were littered with offences, but since he was behaving exactly according to his own idea of normality, he could see nothing unacceptable in this.

At the age of 25, during another stay in prison, Paul decided to go straight. He left prison with good intentions, found himself a job and at first managed to stay on the straight and narrow. It wasn't long, however, before he found himself drawn back to crime, even though he tried not to be tempted. When I spoke to him, he was very disappointed with himself and said that no matter how hard he tried, he kept finding himself committing offences. Although this made him feel bad about himself, when the temptation was there, he just could not resist it.

I wish I could tell you that this story has a happy ending, but I lost contact with Paul many years ago and do not know how his life has turned out. However, over the years, I have given Paul's story a great deal of thought. When I began to understand the workings of the subconscious mind, it became clear to me exactly what his problem was. Even though Paul wanted to stop being drawn to crime, his subconscious mind (inner child) did not. To his subconscious mind, crime was defined as normal behaviour – because this is what it had been programmed with during his first five or six years – and so was safely in his comfort zone. When, as an adult, Paul wanted to break out of his comfort zone, his subconscious mind took every opportunity to draw him back in.

When you think about how deep-rooted and fundamental our subconscious mind is to our entire personality, it is hardly surprising that it is very influential. We all have to contend with the daily tussle with our subconscious mind, but when we understand that it is simply trying to keep us within the boundaries of our own comfort zone, we have taken the first step towards doing something to take control over it.

Sue's comfort zone with food
Another friend of mine – let's call her Sue – has spent the last year or so trying to lose weight – something many of us have struggled with at some time. She has tried every

kind of diet, with the same results: she loses a few pounds at the beginning, but a few weeks later the weight is back on. Then it's on to the next diet regime. She has fallen into the trap of yoyo dieting and is unable to maintain her ideal weight for any length of time. So why is it so difficult for Sue – like many of us – to get into new eating habits and stick to them?

Let's take a careful look at what is happening here. When Sue begins the diet, she really wants to lose weight and is fully motivated. She has the necessary willpower to control her eating habits. She knows that she will feel better and be healthier if she eats well and maintains the right weight for her height and build. The principles are easy enough to understand: eat the right amount of the right foods and she will lose weight. And with the range of healthy food options available these days, there is never even any need for her to feel hungry. Nevertheless, after the first few weeks, or even days, she finds herself drifting back into bad eating habits. Sue's favourite tactic is to move the goal posts. Having decided that she wanted to lose weight for an up-and-coming holiday, she then decides it's for her daughter's graduation ceremony, then for Christmas, then for the new year, and so on.

The problem is, of course, that Sue is obeying her inner child. Her subconscious is telling her that the unhealthy diet she has become used to or has cultivated over the years is what she should be eating. This kind of food is her comfort zone, and it is very difficult to leave it. 'No, you can't have any chocolate or sweets and you must eat plenty of fresh vegetables' isn't what Sue's inner child wants to hear. Sue's initial determination will control the child for a while, but very soon the child's persistence will be rewarded, because it just feels right to go back to your comfort zone.

Jim's comfort zone with keeping fit

Jim's story is another good example of how the subconscious mind sabotages our efforts to instigate change. When Jim first went to the gym he was filled with enthusiasm and energy for his get-fit project. Sure enough, the first few visits were easy, as he raced around the equipment, lifting weights, doing sit-ups and so on, quite possibly overdoing it in his eagerness to succeed. Then, after a while, the novelty wore off. Jim started to accept the feeblest excuses for not going to the gym – 'I have to take the dog for a walk', 'I feel a bit tired' and (an old favourite of many of us) 'I haven't got time'. Of course, just as Jim's initial determination had begun to wear off, his subconscious mind had kicked in, renewing its bid to regain control and pull Jim back into his comfort zone.

Just imagine taking a five-year-old child to the gym with you. At first they may be excited and full of energy, dragging you around the gym and trying out all the equipment. This might continue for two or three visits, but then the child would begin to get bored and start whingeing about having to go. You would end up virtually dragging them there, and while you doggedly followed your keep-fit programme, the child would probably be sitting in the corner sulking.

This is exactly what happens in reality; only it's your inner child that behaves in this way. You don't realise that this is what is going on; you just feel the symptoms. Your enthusiasm wanes, you feel tired, you look for excuses not to go, and the next thing you know, you haven't been for weeks and you regret taking out a gym membership that commits you to the next – very expensive – six months.

Familiar story? I know it's happened to me on more than one occasion. Yet again, it's the subconscious mind dragging us back into our comfort zone – no wonder it is so hard to go forward in life when the most restricting

Your subconscious mind acts just like a child and soon gets bored.

factor is hidden in our own head. But remember, knowing what's going on is the first step towards being able to do something about it.

Jeff and Dave's stories

Another way to explore the notion of the comfort zone is to compare two people with similar upbringings. Jeff and Dave had known each other all their lives. They grew up together on a housing estate in a typical working-class environment. Their birthdays were only three days apart, and as children they were inseparable.

Jeff was the youngest of five children, with two brothers and two sisters. Life was quite hard for them, as their father and mother had separated when Jeff was only five years old, and during the time before the separation the house had been filled with arguments and anger as his parents struggled to cope. Jeff's father had never held down a job for long and spent most of his time drinking and gambling away the family's money on the horses. Money was therefore scarce, and Jeff had to rely on hand-me-down clothes from his older brothers. The family always had enough to eat, but there was no money for life's luxuries, such as holidays, treats or days out. All these factors combined to mean that the primary emotions surrounding Jeff in his formative years were anger, worry, self-pity, hostility, fear and a general sense of having less than everybody else.

As you will now recognise, all these emotions are low-vibrational. Naturally, they contributed hugely to how Jeff felt about himself. He felt that he wasn't as good as most of the other children because they seemed to have lots more than him, so his habitual thought patterns about himself were low-frequency: 'I don't deserve', 'I'm not as good as other people' and 'I can't do anything' were the kind of statements he would unconsciously repeat to himself. This negativity became Jeff's norm. His subconscious mind believed this was what he deserved to be, and it set about ensuring that this was what he got for the rest of his life.

Jeff was a very good soccer player and made the school team, but he found it hard to motivate himself and missed many chances of furthering his progress. He was quite bright but somehow could never be bothered to try hard enough, so he failed most of his exams. He could have made the swimming team but found an excuse so that he didn't have to take part.

When he left school, Jeff found work with an insurance company as a sales representative. He did okay, but somehow he was never going to be one of the high flyers. After a few years in this job he decided that selling insurance was too much like hard work and that he would do much better in a new job, even though some of the other reps were making good money and doing very well. He always had his own reasons for why they did better than him. It was because they had better areas than him or easier policies to sell. One thing was for sure: it was never his fault. So Jeff continued moving from one job to the next over the next few years, not really getting on in any of them, because – according to Jeff – the other reps always had it better in some way. In the end, he put it down to the fact that he just didn't have any luck.

The crucial fact that Jeff wasn't aware of was that he himself was in control of his seeming lack of good fortune. His subconscious mind – programmed to believe that Jeff

Dave and Jeff had totally different outlooks on life: Dave was positive, Jeff was negative.

deserved to stay at a low frequency level – was monitoring his life all the way along. In order to keep him at his frequency level, it 'allowed' him only a very small amount of success – any more would have pushed him into a higher frequency zone. As soon as it looked as if he might become more successful, his subconscious mind kicked in and sabotaged any possibility of that happening. A little voice in Jeff's head would convince him that somebody had it in for him or he never got a fair chance or he should find another job because nobody in his current company appreciated him. This is how our subconscious mind keeps us within the comfort zone that it is programmed for.

Now let's take a look at Dave. Dave was an only child whose parents doted on him. His father was a foreman at the local steel works and his mother a very loving woman who spent her time looking after the family and their home. Dave's home was filled with love and positive energy. He remembers that his parents very rarely argued or had any kind of disagreement. Dave grew up a very happy child, whose parents gave him lots of attention and constantly told him that they loved him. Being an only child, he wanted for nothing. He always had fashionable clothes, and there were holidays abroad every year.

Growing up in this pleasant, loving, high-vibrational environment programmed Dave's subconscious mind to believe that this was the frequency zone in which he belonged. His habitual thought patterns about himself were positive: 'I know I can do it', 'I deserve the best', 'I am as good as anybody'.

Dave was never quite as good at soccer as Jeff, but he worked hard and with conviction, so he progressed further and made it to junior colts level with the local professional soccer club. Dave was not quite as bright as Jeff, but, again, he worked hard and eventually left school with good qualifications. After school, Dave followed Jeff into the insurance business and also became a sales representative. He always came in among the top two or three sales reps in the area. He loved his job, and his attitude impressed the management. He was soon promoted to area sales manager, then a few years later to regional sales director. Dave's life seemed charmed compared to Jeff's; everything always seemed to work out for him.

Jeff and Dave's friendship suffered over the years as their different life paths moved them into different social circles. Of course, they still spoke when they met, but after a while they found they had little in common, and their meetings became more of a passing hello than an in-depth conversation. In fact, Dave's success engendered not a little resentment in Jeff, which, sadly, estranged the two men even further.

Why our vibrational frequency is so important

Looking at Dave and Jeff's lives gives us an idea of how incredibly important our early years are in determining how easy the rest of our life is likely to be. Even though Dave was less talented and not as bright as Jeff, it was still much easier for him to be successful in life than it was for Jeff.

Dave's subconscious programming was of a much higher frequency than Jeff's. His feelings about himself and his own expectations were on a more high-vibrational frequency. He felt better about his abilities, so he had the confidence to try harder; he expected the best, so he impressed others with his positive attitude. All this enabled him to be successful at most of the things that he attempted. His subconscious mind monitored his life and kept him in the higher-frequency zone where it was programmed to believe he should be.

This meant that Dave saw life in a very different way from Jeff. What appeared to be insurmountable obstacles to

Dave had a much higher-frequency upbringing than Jeff, and this was the real difference between them.

Jeff were mere molehills to Dave. In a situation where Jeff's subconscious mind might say, 'That's just my luck; it will never work out for me', Dave's would say 'I'm always lucky; I know this will work for me'. Where Jeff's subconscious might say 'This job is a waste of time; everybody has an insurance policy', Dave's might say, 'I love this job; everybody needs insurance'. At higher frequency levels, life looks and feels completely different than it does at the lower levels. Jeff and Dave had exactly the same job, dealing with the same customers, and they had the same potential for success; the only difference was their vibrational frequency.

By now you will have a very clear idea of how our personal vibrational frequency can control our lives. You will soon begin to learn how high-vibrational thinking can help to change that frequency and put us back in control.

Frequency Variations

Before we move on to looking at how to start raising your vibrational frequency, there is one more issue to consider. That is how our average vibrational frequency changes naturally. Although it is true that the foundations of our subconscious, and therefore our average frequency level, are established at an early stage, our frequency level can and does change in relation to time, the people we interact with and the various challenges life presents us with.

We regularly encounter both high-vibrational and low-vibrational energy from both inside and outside. Here we are going to look at the energy we encounter from outside. How we cope with this on the inside is, of course, vital, so we'll look at this issue at the end of the chapter.

Frequency interaction
How we interact with other people has a major impact on our energy levels on a daily basis. In the case of Jeff and Dave in the previous chapter, we saw that Dave had a fundamentally positive, high-frequency energy, and because of this he made other people feel better too. The management recognised his potential, the customers were more responsive. This is because any interaction with another human being affects your frequency level. If you interact with somebody of a higher frequency, you will have your frequency pulled up; likewise, if you interact

with a person of a lower frequency, you will be dragged down. This is why some people feel very draining to be with, whereas others feel uplifting.

A positive, high-frequency attitude is great to be around.

It's easy to demonstrate this effect just by thinking about a few of the people you know. If you are having a conversation with someone who is up-beat and enthusiastic, there's lots of high-vibrational energy around. You can chat for hours without the conversation lagging. On the other hand, if you are having a conversation with someone who is withdrawn and unhappy, there's so much low-vibrational energy that you may struggle to keep the conversation going. You are being affected by this person's low-vibrational energies – as they are likewise affected by your vibrational frequency.

Let's pursue this a bit further. If you are yourself feeling down while you are trying to cheer someone else up, it will be much harder work. In fact, it's quite likely that you will both ending up crying into your beer! On the other hand, if you are feeling pretty good at the beginning of the conversation, they may pull you down a bit, but it is more likely that you will be able to raise their spirits and help them to feel better.

The more you can be around high-vibrational energy, the more it will benefit your own energy levels on a daily basis. And if you are constantly around high-vibrational people, then the impact can help to stimulate a long-term improvement in your own energies. You really are fundamentally affected by the company you keep.

Places also have a vibrational frequency to which we react. We all have places that we love and others that we find intimidating or uncomfortable. Some towns feel depressing and unwelcoming, whereas other towns feel upbeat and pleasant. Here, we are simply picking up on the collective vibrational frequency of the people who live in a particular place.

Changing energy frequency levels

As we progress through our life, we may find that we achieve success in different things – perhaps our career takes off and we become very good at what we do. This increases and reinforces our good opinion of ourselves, giving us more confidence in our own ability and changing our personal thought patterns. This increase in positive thought patterns means that our personal energy frequency rises. A similar, negative, effect can occur if you have a run of bad luck. If you find the problems you encounter too much to cope with, they are likely to depress your vibrational level.

We all experience natural vibrational fluctuations on a daily basis as we encounter and have to cope with life's everyday events. We have probably all experienced the feeling of being down in the dumps, when our problems seem huge and we can't see a way around them. If we have an interrupted night's sleep and wake up on a rainy day to news of a traffic jam on our route to work on the local radio, it can make things feel even worse. But with a good night's sleep and a ray of sunshine when you open the curtains next morning, you feel a new surge of energy and yesterday's problems diminish. What is happening is that we are simply viewing the same situation from a different frequency level.

Anna's typical day

Let us imagine that during any given day we have 100,000 thoughts going through our mind. These thoughts are influenced by day-to-day activities – people we meet, situations we encounter, whether our favourite team wins or loses, news in the newspapers and so on. The thoughts we have may be high-vibrational or low-vibrational, and each one has an influence on the vibration rate of our personal energy field, speeding it up or slowing it down as we go about our daily activities. Let us take a look at a typical day to give you an idea of how it works.

8.00 a.m.
It's a bright spring morning, the sun is shining, and it feels great to be alive. As Anna throws back the curtains, the sun's rays cascade into the bedroom, illuminating everything in a golden glow. This is one of those days when

she feels on top of the world. The children are relaxed and happy as they get ready for school. Anna's thoughts are **high-vibrational** and she feels content. Her mind is untouched by any of the **low-vibrational** situations that we all encounter every day. At this point of the day, it's fair to assume that her personal energy field is vibrating at a fairly fast rate.

8.30 a.m.

This is a great start, but – hang on – little Lucy is lagging behind and holding everybody up. 'Come on, Lucy. Hurry up or you will be late for school,' shouts Anna. A slight feeling of frustration sweeps over her. This is a **low-vibrational** emotion, and it slows Anna's personal energy field down slightly.

9.00 a.m.

'But it's still a great day,' Anna thinks to herself as she ushers the children into the car and sets off for school. A few jokes on the way ensure a happy and laughter-filled journey so, as this is a **high-vibrational** situation, it speeds up her personal energy field.

9.30 a.m.

The children are safely in school when up strolls Mrs Johnson. 'Oh, no!' Anna says to herself, 'who is she going to be gossiping about today?' Sure enough, away she goes: 'Well I don't know who she thinks she is …' and 'What they need a big car like that for I don't know …'. Now Anna's personal energy field is slowing down as she lends a sympathetic ear to Mrs Johnson and listens to her jealousy, resentment and envy directed at one person after another. The **low-vibrational** conversation is dragging down Anna's energy field. After 15 minutes, Mrs Johnson announces that she has to go, leaving Anna slightly dazed and feeling decidedly grumpy.

Anna's vibrational level is lowered by contact with another person's negative energy.

10.00 a.m.
The journey home is uneventful; a good thing really, because Anna is in no mood for any aggravating drivers. After parking the car, she opens the front door to find a pile of letters waiting for her on the carpet. 'Let's see what we've got here then,' she thinks to herself. 'Gas bill, electricity bill, telephone bill, credit card bill and a couple of junk mail letters. Well, there shouldn't be too much to worry about there.' She decides to make a cup of tea before opening the mail.

First, the gas bill: it's slightly more than she was expecting, but their budget can cope with it. 'I wonder if we have a gas leak? No, we probably left the heating on more than I realised,' she thinks to herself. Suddenly **low-vibrational** thoughts begin to creep into her mind, and she starts to worry, so slowing down her personal energy field.

Next, the electricity bill. That's a lot lower than she expected, which is a nice bonus that makes up for the gas bill. She feels a little uplift, and a small wave of **high-vibrational** joy sweeps through her mind. Up goes her personal energy field.

Next, the credit card statement: not so bad!

But then she opens the telephone bill: £500! 'My goodness, how can that be?' Anxiety takes hold as she scrambles around for the itemised statement. 'I knew it! The Internet! I'll swing for him when he gets home!' A flood of **low-vibrational** emotions hit: worry, fear, anger. Anna's personal energy field plummets as she engages in this **low-vibrational** energy. By now, her personal energy field is slowing right down and she feels terrible. That's all she needed; now she has a headache as well.

11.00 a.m.

Anna spends the rest of the morning fretting over her financial problems and feeling very low indeed. 'Will anything ever go right?' she wonders? Suddenly her **low-vibrational** state is interrupted by the doorbell. As she opens the door, Anna is greeted by a big smile from Jane, her next door neighbour. 'Put the kettle on,' says Jane as she charges by, brimming with confidence and **high-vibrational** energy. 'You look fed up,' she says, catching Anna's miserable face. 'What's wrong?' Well, that's just what Anna needed, and she begins to pour out all her problems. As she fires each one towards Jane, Jane just bats it away with her usual **high-vibrational**, positive outlook. After an hour's conversation, Anna feels decidedly better. Jane has put her problems in perspective, and Anna's personal energy field has shot up. The **low-vibrational** thoughts that weighed heavily on her mind an hour ago now seem trivial, and strangely enough her headache has gone as well. Jane dashes off to her mother's, and Anna decides it's time to do the shopping.

Anna's vibrational level is raised by contact with another person's positive energy.

12.00 noon

The sun is bright (although Anna had failed to notice it during her **low-vibrational** morning). She soon has the car backed out of the drive and is heading towards town. She pulls into the car park. Everything seems rosy again, and her stressful morning feels like a distant memory. Her first stop is the butchers; she joins the queue and waits to be served. The butcher is always very friendly. As soon as he sees Anna, he remarks that she looks younger every time he sees her. Anna feels herself blush, but she is very pleased to receive the compliment and feels uplifted. The **high-vibrational** energy directed towards her has pushed up the frequency of her personal energy field, which also has the effect of making her feel good about herself: more **high-vibrational** thoughts, which drown out any **low-vibrational** thought patterns she normally carries about herself.

12.30 p.m.

Soon the shopping is done, and Anna heads back to the car park, laden down with bags. As she approaches the car, she hears a loud screeching noise heading towards her. She turns to see a car hurtling by at speed. It narrowly misses her, but she drops one of her bags of shopping – eggs, tins and fruit fall everywhere. Anna's heart is pounding at the thought of how close the car came to knocking her down – and not so much as an apology. Her initial feelings are fear and panic, but they are soon followed by frustration and anger. She is fuming! 'How could that idiot drive like that?' she thinks to herself. 'What if the children had been with me?' She decides to report the incident to the police. By this time her personal energy field has plummeted as a result of all this **low-vibrational** energy.

Anna's vibrational level plummets as a result of stress and anger.

2.30 p.m.
After two hours in the police station, Anna is feeling very fed up. The possibility of anything being done about the incident appears to be nil. Anna trudges out. Her personal energy field is now very slow indeed. To compound the situation, she is running late to pick up the children, so she dashes to the school, feeling decidedly down in the dumps. The children are very well behaved on the journey home, as they immediately sense Anna's bad mood. Once in the house, she chases them upstairs to do their homework while she makes the tea, her mind racing with the day's

events. Bills, Mrs Johnson's gossiping, the car park incident ... Anna wallows in **low-vibrational** thoughts. Her personal energy field is slowing down even further. She feels really depressed. 'Why is life so stressful?' and 'Nothing seems to go right' are the kind of thoughts racing around in her head. The children avoid her, as they can see her bad mood has not lifted. Indeed, Anna's mind is pulsating with anger, which she is ready to direct at her husband when he gets home.

Anna prepares to direct her low-vibrational mood towards her husband.

5.00 p.m.
'Hello, darling!' shouts John, as he opens the front door. Anna is ready for him, fired up and angry. As she turns to face him, her mind is racing with what she is going to say, but he stops her dead in her tracks. 'For you,' he says, handing her a dozen red roses. 'I've booked a table at our favourite restaurant to celebrate my promotion! From now on it's only the best for us. My salary has gone up 20 per cent and they've thrown in a company car. Now, what is it you wanted to say?' All of a sudden Anna's anger and fear vanish; the good news from her husband has dissipated her

negativity. Suddenly, she is feeling good, and her personal energy field races up. 'It was nothing really,' she blurts out. 'Anyway, let's celebrate! What marvellous news!' The children come running down the stairs – they sense that the atmosphere has changed from **low-vibrational** to **high-vibrational** energy. Suddenly, the house is filled with happiness; Anna's bad day seems like a distant nightmare. How on earth had she allowed herself to get so down?

7.00 p.m.

A short while later, as she lies soaking in a hot bubble bath with a wonderful night in front of her, Anna thinks back over her day and begins to recognise how she became the victim of her own thinking. Every time she allowed a thought to grab hold of her and control her without offering any resistance, she became the victim of all the **low-vibrational** energy that had come her way. But, she realises, she did not have to engage with these **low-vibrational** energies quite so eagerly. If she could have detached herself from them, her personal energy field would not have been quite so affected. She didn't have to take it so much to heart when Mrs Johnson started resenting and envying everybody. She didn't have to let the bills get her down – she and John had always managed to get by. She didn't need to let the feelings of fear, panic, anger and frustration overwhelm her when the car screeched past her in the car park. And she didn't need to mull over all of these **low-vibrational incidents** for the rest of the afternoon, thus slowing down her personal energy field even further.

Anna's energy field

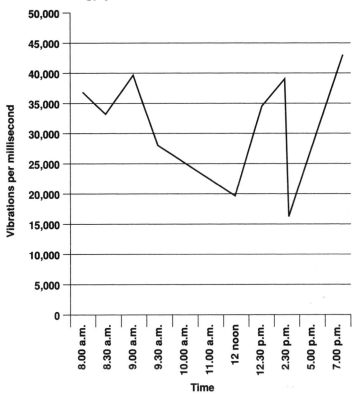

Fluctuations in Anna's energy field throughout the day.

As you can see from the graph, Anna's personal energy field has fluctuated throughout the day as she alternated between positive and negative thoughts – from a low point of 17,000 vibrations per millisecond at 2.30 p.m., when she had just left the police station, to a high point of 48,000 vibrations per millisecond at 7 p.m., as she lay in a hot bath with only positive thoughts in her mind. Remember, the faster our personal energy field vibrates, the better we feel, because we are closer to the high-vibrational energy of love.

Coping with negative energy

It doesn't matter what is pulling you down – the gas bill, the TV breaking down, the children stressing you out. You cannot avoid the low-vibrational energy in your environment; this is the very nature of life. What does matter is how you choose to react to these low-frequency attacks, because you can have some control over how much these situations and events affect you.

I recall an incident in my office in which one of the administrators had had a particularly stressful morning dealing with complaints of various sorts. This low-frequency energy had given her a headache. Then the telephone rang and she found out that she had just won quite a large amount of money. She happily passed on the story of her good fortune to the rest of the staff. A little later, I asked her if she still had a headache. To her amazement, she replied that it had completely disappeared. You see, sometimes even headaches can be instantly cured if you can find a way to lift your personal energy vibration.

On another occasion, a boy I know called Jordan lost his brand-new mobile phone. He was distraught, as his father had just bought him this expensive present. When he realised that he had lost his phone, his whole day looked completely different: one minute he was happy and enjoying himself and the next he was inconsolable. His mind had suddenly become filled with low-vibrational emotions: worry, fear, anger, frustration, disappointment. This had the effect of pulling down his energy frequency. It was several days before Jordan recovered and moved back up to his normal frequency level. That's how powerful negative energy can be.

If negative energy is so powerful, you need an equally powerful weapon to use against it – and that's high-vibrational thinking.

Taking Control

So let's briefly recap. Energy is vibrating all around us. The energy of love is high-vibrational; the energy of fear is low-vibrational. The closer we can stay to the vibration that we call love, the better we will succeed in all aspects of our lives.

Most of life's problems exist at the lower frequency levels, so if you are focused on low-vibrational energy, you are likely to be ill more often, end up in more arguments, have more trouble with your car or your computer, find it harder to get a job or succeed at work, and experience problems at school or with the children. In fact, everything will be much more difficult.

High-vibrational thinking is a way of learning to dismiss low-vibrational thoughts and replace them with high-vibrational thoughts. It makes absolute sense to try to think in a more high-vibrational way, because this puts you in control. And being able to control your thoughts and feelings will help you to change your life. You can learn to use high-vibrational thinking in every aspect of your life. You deserve the positive energies of love, happiness and joy in your life just as much as anyone else.

Just being aware of high-vibrational thinking is the first step to taking control of your energy field, as it enables you to understand what is happening in your mind and to appreciate that control is lacking. Once you have taken that first step, it won't be long before you automatically begin to assess situations in terms of energy and put HVT into practice without thinking about it. This makes a welcome change from being controlled by negative energies, tossed around like a rag doll in the wind.

Reprogramming our subconscious

There are two elements in making HVT work for you: one deals with your fundamental energy levels, and the other deals with how you react to the changing energy levels around you.

The influences we experience during our formative years help to establish our normal vibrational frequency and define our comfort zone: our fundamental feelings about ourselves and the kind of life we believe we deserve. Throughout our life, our subconscious mind monitors our feelings and actions so that we stay within the boundaries of our comfort zone – whether that is good for us or not. If we try to move away from that comfort zone, we are engaging in a battle for control – and it's a battle that we usually lose.

There is another way – one that avoids the battle and enables us to take control. The answer is to re-programme your subconscious mind and so change the boundaries of your comfort zone.

Let's take the dieting example that we looked at on pages 26–7. While your comfort zone is chips, chips and more chips, any diet will be a huge struggle that is almost doomed to failure, because you will be constantly drawn back to your comfort zone. But if you change the boundaries of your comfort zone, your subconscious mind will monitor what you eat to keep you at the newly programmed weight that is now within your comfort zone. You will be able to change your eating habits, with the result that you are attracted to a more healthy diet of less fattening foods. If you look at those people who have dieted successfully and lost lots of weight permanently, you will generally find that they have also successfully re-programmed their subconscious mind.

If it's improved fitness you are trying to achieve, the principles are just the same. While your comfort zone is an evening with your feet up in front of the TV, that is what your subconscious will be pulling you towards.

HVT is a way of re-programming that does away with the need for an iron will. This book will show you how to achieve that re-programming. The first step towards change is to understand how your mind works and accept the power of the subconscious mind. Once you appreciate this, you can begin to move forward and make plans for a new and exciting future.

Of course, once you have re-programmed your

With HVT you can re-train your inner child.

subconscious into a new comfort zone, it will start to form new and more positive habits. If you have an established habit of taking regular exercise, when you miss your exercise for some reason, you will feel tired and drained. It's almost as if you are addicted to exercise and without it you feel down. This, again, is your subconscious pushing you to stick to the comfort zone – but in this case, of course, the comfort zone is healthy, so the subconscious is a force for good.

So you can see that your subconscious can be programmed for success or failure, and it will use all its powerful influence to maintain whatever it is programmed for. If we can re-programme our subconscious for success, clearly this is the answer to many of our problems. This book will show you how to do just that – to change your subconscious comfort zone in relation to the specific problems and issues that are relevant to you.

Start changing now

You don't have to wait until you have read the whole book to make changes in your life. You can start making changes straightaway. Start by dealing with the energy fluctuations you encounter on a daily basis and how you react to them.

Remember the outline of Anna's fairly ordinary day (see pages 38–45). Look at it again and you will see how Anna allowed herself to be engaged by the energies around her rather than taking control of her own energy field. When she encountered low-vibrational energy from outside, or when her own emotions were low-vibrational – both things we can't always avoid – she allowed herself to be dragged down and ended up feeling even worse. You are probably just the same. Now that you realise that by engaging with low-vibrational thoughts you are only going to damage yourself by dragging down your personal energy field, you can start to implement changes that will make an immediate difference to your life.

Don't engage with low-vibrational energy
The crucial thing is not to engage emotionally with low-vibrational energy, because it is when you become emotionally attached to negativity that you are most damaged. Your personal energy frequency will plummet and move you into a much more difficult frequency zone.

You can now recognise low-vibrational energy as anything that pulls you down and makes you feel negative: anger, disappointment, envy, spite and so on. When you encounter that kind of energy, the secret is to remain calm and to let the negative energy pass over you without buying into it. Try to visualise the energy moving away from you and disappearing, rather than hanging on to it and engaging with it mentally. The principle is very simple: recognise it and reject it.

Start right now. The next time you find low-vibrational thoughts coming into your mind, let them go. You almost certainly won't succeed straightaway; it will take a little practice, but even the first time you try it, you will feel some impact. Then, every time you succeed, it will become easier and more automatic to reject negativity. If you stick at it and follow the specific guidance in this book, you will get better at it every day.

Take bills as an example. If you have a gas bill that is higher than you expected, you obviously have to do something about it. But worrying is not going to make the bill any smaller; nor is it going to get it paid. If you put aside the worry, you have more energy to think about positive things that will help you to solve the actual problem of paying the bill. Your mind will be able to focus on the options: you can dip into your savings, contact the supplier and arrange to pay it off gradually, turn down the heating thermostat so it doesn't happen again – or whatever.

Concentrate on the present

So visualising negative energy draining away will help. Another very simple way to handle low-vibrational thought patterns is to concentrate on the present.

We all spend too much of our time thinking about the past or the future. Our minds tend to dwell on something that has happened or something that might happen until this becomes a habit that is difficult to break. In fact, we are often scarcely aware that we are doing this.

It is all too easy to dwell on a low-vibrational event that has happened in the past: the time we struggled to meet a payment date; the time someone shouted at us or let us down. We keep running it over and over again in our minds like some kind of loop-tape action replay. The result of replaying thoughts of anger, frustration, disappointment, fear or uncertainty is that our personal frequency level is dragged down even more, pulling us down into a negative zone.

Likewise, we may focus our attention on a future negative event that may never happen: the cold we are sure we are going to catch, the redundancy that is bound to come, and so on. Similarly, the effect is to lower our frequency level, leeching away all our positive energy.

The past is gone and we cannot change it. Dwelling on its negative energies will only drag us down. We simply need to learn from it and move on. The future is not here yet; worrying about something that may or may not happen will only drag down your personal energy field, making life much harder in the process.

If you can avoid this time trap and think in the present, you will find that your energy levels remain high. By being alert to this pitfall, you can train your mind to recognise when you are about to fall into the trap. Then you simply stop and remind yourself to concentrate on the present. If you have a problem, look at what you can do now to solve it in the best possible way.

Use high-vibrational thinking to clear your mind of

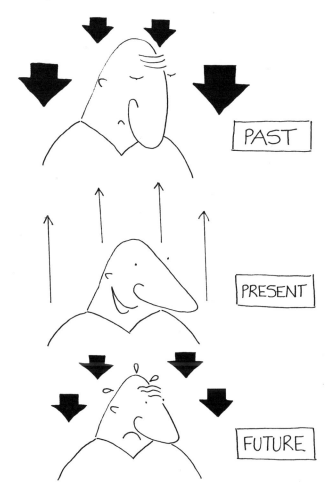

Dwelling on the past and worrying about the future is a complete waste of energy. Stay focused in the present if you want to get the best out of your life.

clutter and stay focused in the present moment; then you are ready to handle life to the best of your ability.

Take one step at a time

There will be times when you don't manage to dismiss low-vibrational thoughts altogether. Don't worry about it – for worrying is in itself hanging on to low-vibrational energies. Look at what you did achieve; tell yourself how much better you did it than last time; congratulate yourself and move on. Before long you will find that you are more and more in control. This means that your personal energy field will not slow down as easily next time you encounter low-vibrational energy, and you won't have to spend every day on a mental rollercoaster ride.

Remember, you are more in control than you realise. Your thoughts create your reality, so if you fill your mind with high-vibrational thoughts, you will have a more positive, enjoyable and fulfilling life. You can take control of your own energy.

Your Potential

'We are unlimited beings, experiencing life in a physical body subject to the ceilings of our imagination.' Bill Hicks

Now you understand how HVT works, you are almost certainly beginning to see many ways of applying it to your life. Here we are going to examine specifically how HVT can make you feel good about yourself. Then we will be looking at a complete six-week programme in which you will be putting your new-found knowledge into practice.

To realise your full potential, you need to attune your personal energy field to the frequency of love on a permanent basis. This means both that your own comfort zone will be high-vibrational and that you will have learned to deal with low-vibrational energies in your surroundings so that you remain in a high-vibrational energy field all the time – or as much of the time as is humanly possible.

Staying in a high-vibrational zone is the goal – and we are all fully engaged in pursuing this, whether we realise it or not, because whatever happens in our lives, we all want to be happy. Indeed, everything we do is focused on this single aim. Our whole life is geared towards this deep-seated desire to be at one with the energy that we call love.

Of course, we have to accept that we live in the real world and we all have to confront and deal with problems to a greater or lesser extent. It is unrealistic to expect total happiness all the time, but it is realistic to aspire to make our life as good as we can possible make it. We can make things better – much better – for ourselves every day, and we can start to do this straight away by harnessing high-vibrational thinking.

A high-vibrational revelation

If you are in a low patch in your life, which is quite likely since you are reading this book, you may be thinking, 'It's easy for him to say this. He doesn't have to cope with my problems.' That may be so, but it's not true that I don't know how it feels to be down or have never had to turn my life around.

Let me give you an example. Some years ago I was going through a particularly stressful time and I was feeling very low. I was at a point in my life when I was desperately searching for an answer to my problems – just the usual ones that we all encounter but which can sometimes seem huge and insurmountable. I was having a particular problem sleeping and was becoming increasingly tired and irritable. Each night I would lie awake turning all my troubles over in my mind; the more I tried to tell myself that I needed to sleep, the more awake I became.

Then one night I had an amazing experience. Eventually, after tossing and turning as usual, I fell into a deep sleep. The next thing I knew, the sun was shining through the blinds and I could hear the birds singing. For some completely inexplicable reason, I felt absolutely great and on top of the world. The huge problems that had so engulfed me the previous evening now seemed trivial. I had never felt better in my life and I set off to work in an almost dream-like state. The world had taken on a whole new and exciting aspect. Everything looked different to me: the grass was greener than I had ever noticed before; the sky was an incredible blue, somehow brighter and deeper than I had ever seen it.

When I got to work the amazement continued. Every person I encountered seemed to have bright shining eyes, as if some kind of energy was pouring out from deep within them. Their faces were shining with joy, and they all looked so beautiful. I remember feeling such compassion for everybody. It was almost as though I wanted to take care of everyone.

This incredible feeling lasted for about one month, and it is an experience that I will never forget. I was so disappointed when my old feelings slowly began to reappear, and I desperately tried to cling on to this amazing and beautiful feeling of unconditional love that I had inexplicably come across, but unfortunately the 'real' world came back and reclaimed me.

At the time I never fully appreciated or understood what had taken place; I just knew that something quite profound had happened to me. It was almost impossible to explain my amazing experience to other people. Since I didn't really understand it myself, I couldn't put it into words, so I simply pushed it to the back of my mind. It wasn't until some years later, as my understanding of high-vibrational thinking grew, that I appreciated what had really happened.

Somehow, for one month of my life, I had come close to resonating at the same frequency as the energy that we call love. I don't know why this happened to me; I just know that it did. This incredible experience then became my life's goal: I wanted to get that feeling back, and I had to find a way to understand it before I could do that. That is what led me to define high-vibrational thinking. Once it all fell into place, I felt I truly understood the world in terms of energy, and I saw how this understanding could help everyone in the search for higher self-esteem and happiness.

Finding enlightenment

My feelings now about that amazing month of my life are that I had experienced what it would be like to attain enlightenment. This, of course, is the ultimate goal of many a seeker of wisdom and happiness, and you will find reference to it in many books and teachings.

My personal view of enlightenment now is that to attain it you must reach a state of being where you have no low-vibrational thoughts or feelings in your mind. You are so free of negativity that your personal energy field rises accordingly and you bask in the frequency of love.

As I look back on that time, I feel I have now come to a clear understanding of what actually happened. The stress and pressure I felt at that time had somehow triggered off a reaction in my mind. This reaction took the form of letting go completely of all of the low-vibrational thoughts and feelings I was carrying, which allowed my personal energy frequency to rise. This releasing of negativity from my mind allowed my frequency to hit the heights, and I was able to resonate closer to the frequency of love than I ever had before. The feeling was indescribably beautiful and, on reflection, I realise that it is what we are all really seeking. The only thing holding us back from it is our low-vibrational thoughts and feelings. If we can dispense with these, our personal energy frequency will rise, moving us closer to the frequency of love.

But this is real life!

'Easier said than done,' you are probably thinking – and, of course, you are right. The fact that something clicked in my mind overnight still gave me only a limited insight into that high-vibrational world. After that, I've had to work at it in the same way as anyone else. But I have worked at it and it did work! And it can do for you. It is not beyond any one of us to put HVT to work in our life and make it better

– and understanding the process is a major step towards achieving that. Once you can look at yourself and your relationships with others in terms of energy, you can see very clearly how the whole process works, and this is very empowering. To perform at your peak, in whatever it is you are doing, you must attain as high a personal frequency rate as possible. A sportsperson has to play 'in the zone' to achieve peak performance; a karate expert has to attain a state of 'no mind' to break through piles of bricks. It's all the same thing: working to attain a state of consciousness without negativity. You have no doubts; you just know you can do it.

Judging your potential

Every one of us has unique qualities, strengths and weaknesses. Within us is the potential to use those strengths to the full and minimise those weaknesses, but we will only be able to realise 100 per cent of our potential if we work at it.

Of course, our individual potential is – much the same as we are – completely unique. Only a very few of us have the innate potential to be, say, a nuclear physicist, the Prime Minister of Great Britain or the President of the United States of America. Most of us would be content with much less lofty achievements: we want to be good parents, have a rewarding job and progress to a better one. While a few of us may have the potential to be a top tennis or rugby player, many will be happy to achieve a place in a local club team, and yet more will be content to be able to kick a ball round the park.

Are we achieving our potential?

What our individual potential is doesn't matter. What does matter is how close we are to achieving it. The one thing we can be pretty sure of is that 99 per cent of us are not coming anywhere near realising our potential. I know for certain that this applies to me. I always feel that I could achieve more in whatever it is that I am doing – there's always a little bit more to reach for. There is huge room for improvement in just about every area of our lives for almost every one of us.

Why do we fall short?

If we are all falling short of reaching our potential in just about every area of our lives, the million-dollar question is why? I think the answer lies in the lack of a simple understanding of the mechanics of how to handle low-vibrational energy. You don't achieve your potential without working for it; it doesn't happen overnight. But if you don't have effective strategies for maximising your potential, all the work you put in may be wasted. Put simply, you can expend a lot of energy digging a hole, but if it's in the wrong place, all that energy is wasted.

High-vibrational thinking offers you a fundamental understanding of how you can maximise your potential. This will help you to do better at home, at work and in your relationships with other people. The result will be that you feel happier and more fulfilled. In short, you'll feel great about yourself.

Making Small Changes with HVT

I believe that HVT offers a new perspective on our own self-esteem and how we interact with each other. It offers a positive solution to the problem of low self-esteem and – what follows – low achievement.

Learning to think in terms of HVT is the way to a happier and more fulfilling life. Once you begin to look at your life in relation to energy, living it effectively suddenly becomes a less daunting prospect, as you now have the element of control that you previously lacked. HVT will become a way of life for you, as it has already for many people, and the principles of HVT will enable you to handle your life in a much more productive and beneficial way.

This new-found ability will become an automatic response, and you will find yourself changing as a person almost without noticing it. Many HVT students have realised the impact that HVT has had upon their lives only when they have met up with relatives or old friends that they hadn't seen for some time. These friends and relatives have been astonished at the changes in them and amazed that something so simple can have such a dramatic impact. This, of course, makes the friend or relative eager to learn more. This is how news of HVT is spread. HVT truly is a self-development tool that works – and, once you have made it a part of your life, it works with very little conscious effort on your part.

The missing piece

My own experience of the many other self-development books and theories is considerable, as I spent the 20 years before I discovered HVT reading and learning about them. While I found many enlightening and helpful, I always felt that something was missing. I believe that HVT is that missing piece of the jigsaw and that an understanding of HVT is essential as the foundation stone of all your other self-development strategies.

The first affirmation

The first step in raising your self-esteem and feeling great about yourself is affirming that you are going to change your life and that you can and will do so if you persevere. Keep reminding yourself that you are going to change your life for the better. You are great and you are going to feel good about yourself and realise your full potential. Write this affirmation on a piece of paper and stick it on the fridge door or keep it in your pocket. You can even write it on the back of your hand. Just keep reminding yourself all the time.

Keep away from low-frequency people

The second vital step on the way to a high-vibrational future is to learn to recognise low-vibrational people and avoid them. You now know what to look out for: anyone whose company makes you feel down, lacking in energy or fed up. A person who makes you feel drained when you are with them is sapping your personal energy. People we enjoy being with should make us feel good about ourselves. If someone you are around makes you start to question your own abilities or lose your self-confidence, this is not a good sign. Be very careful of so-called friends who seem to be lowering your energy levels or making you feel depressed or lethargic.

What can you do about this? As far as possible, try to avoid such people. Start to make plans that don't include them. Talk to other, more up-beat people and make arrangements to meet with them. You will find that their high-vibrational energy will help you to build up your own energy levels. It may be difficult to begin with, so start with small actions that will be effective but not too noticeable. For example, tag along with the lively crowd when you take your coffee break. Each time you score a small victory, it will increase your confidence, raise your energy levels and help you to cope better next time.

Let comments pass you by

There are times when other people's comments can undermine the self-confidence we have built up. If someone makes a negative comment about you – that you are not up to a job, or even something minor like your hair looks a mess – recognise the comment as low-vibrational and let it pass you by. Don't think about it; certainly don't latch on to it and turn it over in your mind. Don't believe it; don't engage emotionally with it. You don't want anything to do with low-vibrational thinking.

Try to imagine such comments as a physical object, perhaps a tennis ball, that is thrown at you but that you can easily avoid by stepping out of the way so that it bounces harmlessly behind you. You may not find this easy to do the first time, but keep at it and it will get easier every time. If a different image works better for you, then use that. You might envisage the negative person as firing a *Star Trek*-style laser stun-gun, but you are protected by an invisible energy shield, and the ray bounces harmlessly off you. It's just imagination; anything goes!

Return to sender

Another very effective visualisation exercise to stop other
people making you feel negative about yourself is to
imagine a huge mirror between you and the other person.
If they say something derogatory, imagine that the low-
vibrational energy is hitting the mirror and bouncing right
back at them.

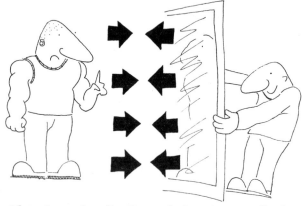

*The mirror visualisation technique is very effective
in repelling negative energy.*

This visualisation has a double impact. Not only does
the mirror protect you from the harmful low-vibrational
energy, but it also returns the energy to the person who
created it so that they have to deal with it. The *Star Trek*
laser image works well here too – the offending person has
to endure the injury they were trying to inflict on you.

Down in the dumps

A similar principle applies in times when you feel down in
the dumps. We all know that when we are fed up, things
look different. Life is a lot bleaker from this perspective.
Small problems seem to grow out of proportion; everything
seems more difficult to cope with. Then, perhaps after a

good night's sleep, a solution is offered, our energy levels pick up and we gain a better sense of proportion. When you are feeling down, try to let go of the negatives rather than hanging on to them. Concentrate on keeping on moving ahead. Life will go much more smoothly for you and your self-esteem will remain higher than if you give in to negative thinking.

Stand up for yourself

Once you have started to use the techniques above, you will soon find your energies increasing. Don't stop there! Keep on telling yourself that you are going to change for the better, and things will keep on getting better. The more you can avoid low-vibrational energy and be around people with high-vibrational energy, the easier it will be to generate your own high-vibrational energy. Then you are really in charge!

When you have gained a little more confidence, start to speak up for yourself. Don't be frightened to state your opinion; you have just as much right to your view as anyone else. Practise telling people what you think. Enjoy it when they notice a change in you and are impressed that you are speaking up.

Turn the conversation on its head

Another useful technique is to practise changing the direction of a conversation if it is making you feel down in any way. You can learn a lot about this from politicians on the television! If the interviewer asks them a question they don't want to answer, they just start talking about something else. If you are with people who you feel are draining you of your high-vibrational energy by talking about negative subjects, being critical, moaning or pouring out all their problems, don't let them do it. Instead of listening to their negativity, interrupt politely and start talking about something more positive.

Stand tall and smarten up

It may sound odd, but you can actually use your physical
stance and appearance to help you feel better about
yourself. Try this experiment. Think about yourself in your
oldest gardening clothes, with no make-up on (assuming
you wear it), your hair in a mess and a spot on your chin.
How does that make you feel? Now smarten yourself up in
your mind: your best clothes, newly washed hair and a big
smile. See yourself standing up tall, with your chin up and
your shoulders back. Take a few deep breaths in and out.
Feel better? That's not just who you could be; that's who
you can be now!

Take that bit of extra care about your clothes and
appearance. You don't have to try to be a fashion icon; just
make sure your clothes are clean and tidy. Clean your
fingernails and wash and brush your hair. Look at yourself
in the mirror and tell yourself how good you look. It's all
about raising those energy levels, and small things like this
count. Stand tall, look people straight in the eye and
breathe deeply. It will make a real difference.

Let Go of the Past

Putting the techniques in the previous chapters into practice will have slowly but surely built your self-esteem by encouraging you to think in high-vibrational ways. Now you are ready for the next phase.

As we discussed earlier, we all have our own personal comfort zone, and our subconscious mind is programmed to keep us within these self-imposed boundaries. To make significant improvements in our life, we must change those boundaries and come to believe that we deserve more love (high-vibrational energy). In order to do this we have to start having fewer low-vibrational thoughts about ourselves and other people. This is something that can be achieved by carrying out a series of practical exercises daily. By doing them we are quite simply exchanging slow vibrational thought patterns for fast vibrational thought patterns, which will have the effect of increasing the frequency of our personal energy field.

We need to get used to living in a higher frequency zone, which means in effect reprogramming our subconscious. This will take a little time – it took me six months – but the changes you make will be permanent. Once you have achieved your first goals, you may feel that they are all you desire, in which case well done! On the other hand, they may have inspired you to want more, in which case simply continue the programme.

Today is the first day

Everybody faces certain challenges in their lives, and these can take many different forms – a difficult childhood, a serious accident, a divorce, the death of a loved one, the loss of a job, being bullied at school, parental divorce while you were young. Indeed, no-one's life challenges will be exactly the same as anyone else's. For our purposes, however, their nature does not matter; what does matter is how we handle them. We can either allow them to destroy us or we can fight back and let them be the making of us. It's a simple choice.

If you hold on to the low-frequency events in your past, they will drag down your personal energy frequency permanently, and you will never be free to move into that high-vibrational zone where you feel really good about yourself. You must let go of all the low-frequency energy associated with your life so far, as you cannot move forward until you have made this decision.

If you are fortunate enough not to have had a major challenge in your life so far, you can skip the next sections and move straight on to Making the Commitment (page 100).

The emotions surrounding your life challenges

Think carefully about all the events in your life that you see as challenges and then list them. These might include:

▸ An unhappy childhood
▸ The loss of a sibling or parent
▸ Being bullied
▸ A parental divorce
▸ Moving away from your home at a crucial time in your life
▸ Failing an important exam
▸ A divorce

When you have completed your list, write down all the low vibrational feelings you associate with these events, such as anger, hatred, self-pity and so on. Remember, these are the low-vibrational thoughts and feelings that are damaging your life. When your list is complete, you will be able to see the negative feelings and emotions that are causing you the most problems, and this will help you to be more aware of them the next time they occupy your mind.

Events	Emotions
. . . .	. . . .
. . . .	. . . .
. . . .	. . . .
. . . .	. . . .
. . . .	. . . .
. . . .	. . . .
. . . .	. . . .
. . . .	. . . .
. . . .	. . . .
. . . .	. . . .
. . . .	. . . .

When you do encounter these emotions again – and you will – recognise them and take a step back from them. Tell yourself very firmly that these are low-vibrational emotions and you do not want to engage with them any more. We will talk more about how to disengage from low-vibrational feelings in the next chapter.

Forgiveness
Look at your list and make a commitment to forgive anybody who you feel may be responsible for your challenge. You need to do this because, as you now know, holding on to hurt and bitterness is only damaging you, and your personal energy frequency will suffer.

Resentment is a low-vibrational energy; it cannot benefit you. Let it go.

Why this will set you free

If we take a look at all of this in terms of HVT, it becomes a lot easier to understand. Let's take, for example, somebody who had a difficult childhood in which they received little affection. A lack of love almost always results in the child growing up to have a low opinion of themselves because their subconscious comes to the conclusion that if their parents didn't love them, they must not deserve any love. This negative thought pattern will be imprinted on their mind and constantly circulate to become their subconscious programming – their comfort zone. It is easy to see that the result of years of living with this habitual thought will be to keep their personal energy frequency vibrating at the lower levels. This ensures a much more difficult life, as life at the lower frequencies is always fraught with problems.

This programming will affect the person's whole outlook on life, be it at work, in relationships or in their social life. If they remain locked in their low-vibrational mode, blaming the past, blaming other people and constantly feeling sorry for themselves, the vicious circle will be complete, and their self-pity will serve to keep them in this low-vibrational prison.

This is why accepting and letting go of the past is so important. It is the key to releasing the negative thought patterns that are so tremendously damaging. It is vital to forgive anybody you may be holding responsible for your current situation. Remember, they too were subject to the limitations of their upbringing and also had to face challenges in life. Let go of any low-vibrational thoughts and move forward into your future.

A formidable challenge

If you're thinking that it's hard to let go of what has happened in your past, you're right! But it is possible. You can do it.

I learnt a valuable lesson in acceptance a number of years ago when I met and became friends with a man who had spent most of his life in a wheelchair. My friend was a boisterous and energetic 12-year-old when he had the accident that changed his life. Severe injuries kept him in hospital for several years, during which time he had to learn to accept that he would never walk again – something far more difficult than most of us will ever have to face. He tussled with many demons and came to the conclusion that this event would either break him or make him. Thankfully, he had the strength of character to choose the latter. Today he is the life and soul of the party and always upbeat and happy. His philosophy is 'accept your lot and move on' because to dwell on his misfortune would condemn him to a low-frequency existence for his entire life. Amazingly, he draws his inspiration from his time in hospital, when he met people far worse off than him but who still managed to remain happy and positive.

It would have been so easy for my friend to fall into the trap of feeling sorry for himself, thinking 'why me?', but thankfully he chose not to go that route, and he continues to be an inspiration to the people around him.

The secret of now!

It is *now* that is important. Let go of the past – it's over and you cannot change it. Don't worry too much about the future either – it may never come, and, in any event, dealing with the present is the best way to set things to work out for the best. Focus on the present moment and make it as good as it can be. You are fully responsible for your life and this is your opportunity to take control.

Face Your Fears

'Your fears are like fences: you have to jump over them to find new territory.' Anon

In the previous chapter we identified some of the emotions that held you back in the past. It is more than likely that, in one form or another, fear was one of them. In this chapter we're going to look in a little more detail at facing up to your fears – and conquering them.

The first thing to remember is that you don't have to face up to all your fears at once. If you were confronted with a pile of sand and had to move it out of your way, you wouldn't expect to be able to pick it up and shift it in one go. You would have to get a shovel and keep digging until it had all been moved. Similarly, you won't transform all your fears overnight. But you will make changes gradually and effectively until you clear your way to a new belief in yourself. The second thing to remember is that now you understand HVT, you have unlocked a powerful weapon in your programme of change – a seriously strong and sturdy shovel!

Facing your fears is a very powerful element in reprogramming your subconscious mind, improving your self-esteem and making you feel good about yourself.

Stuck in the low zone

When you encounter something that has been difficult for you in the past, your subconscious recognises it as being outside its comfort zone. It may not be the actual event that is the problem but rather the emotion it generates. If you have low self-esteem, you may feel anxious about anything from a visit to the dentist to asking someone out on a date, making a telephone call about a job interview, sitting an exam or giving a speech. This anxiety can be very restricting, and can even grow to such an extent that it dominates and controls our life. Remember that any low-vibrational thoughts, if allowed to persist, will generate more low-vibrational energy to pull you down even further.

If you are in this situation, you may have so little self-esteem that you feel you cannot even attempt anything new. Thus you are well and truly stuck in the low-frequency zone.

Face your fears and you can beat them

How many times have you seen this? A person is terrified of getting up and having a go on the karaoke machine. Eventually, egged on by their friends, they push themselves through their fear and get up to sing. All of a sudden, you can't get the microphone out of their hands. They have faced and overcome a fear – thus taking a major step forward in changing their conditioning programme – and the experience has made them feel elated. Facing your fears is a marvellous way of improving your life, and it helps you to believe that you are deserving of the energy that we call love.

Face the fear and beat it, and you will feel elated.

My story

I once had a job selling magazines on the street to the
general public. This was something new to me and I found
the prospect very daunting. Every morning on the way to
work, a feeling of dread welled up inside me. It was awful
thinking about approaching people all day and asking if
they would like to buy a magazine; I really hated doing it.
But as the other salesmen were making a success of it and I
had a family to provide for, I was left with no option but to
battle through my anxiety. By the end of each day, when I
had sold enough magazines, I did feel good, but the next
morning the fear was back again. I struggled for six
months before the feeling of dread completely left me.

I well remember a day in late December – the worst I
ever had to face. I was in a run-down area of a north-
eastern town. It was absolutely freezing and snow was
falling sporadically. My sales target was 120 magazines
each day, and I had to hit this target just to earn enough
for my family and me to exist. I started at 9 a.m., and by
2.30 p.m. I had sold just 14 magazines, and that was
without stopping for a break. It would be dark by 4.30 p.m.
and I would have to finish, so I was way behind target and
very disillusioned. People were rushing past me, huddling
their coats tightly around them to keep out the bitter cold.
I asked one person after another but to no avail. I
understood why they were refusing me: it was nearly
Christmas and they needed their spare cash; it was too cold
to stop and talk; it was late and people wanted to get
home. All the odds seemed stacked against me. It was
obvious that selling magazines was just not going to work.
I felt so dejected that I decided to give up and go home.

But as I slowly turned to walk away, I changed my
mind. I decided I would not give up. I didn't care what it
took, I was prepared to stay until midnight if I had to, but
I would not give up. I still don't know where this sudden

determination came from; something just clicked in my head. I had made a decision and that was it.

I saw a lady approaching me, hands full of shopping and coat clasped tightly around her. I said, 'Excuse me, but would you care for a magazine?' Her face beamed a huge smile, and she replied, 'Of course I would.' That set the tone for what I can only describe as an amazing two hours. By 4.30 p.m. I had sold my quota of magazines: 106 sales in the last two hours!

Unbelievable? It seemed so then, but now I understand what was going on. I was afraid of doing well. I had to face up to my subconscious and break away from the programming that told me I did not deserve success. Each day when I went to work I was engaging my subconscious in battle. By selling lots of magazines I was earning more money than I was used to, and this was taking me out of my comfort zone. My subconscious did not like this, and so I spent each day tussling with it as it tried to talk me out of selling them. But all its convincing reasons were valid only within my comfort zone.

It turned out that all I needed was a change in attitude. The justifications for my inevitable failure were all in my mind. I was in control much more than I realised.

How to tackle your fears

It is easy to say that you need to tackle your fears, but how do you make a start? Well, first of all, you need to identify them. They might include anything from going out for a meal on your own to engaging a stranger in conversation. Then you need to look at each of your fears one by one, starting with the one that feels easiest, and draw up a plan of action to confront it. You may need to make some special arrangements in order to do this. If, for example, one of your fears is doing a parachute jump, you will need to give yourself a few weeks to make arrangements to meet it. If you feel a little apprehensive at the thought of facing one of your fears, ask a friend to be there to offer support.

My fears	*Action plan to overcome them*
. . . .	. . . .
. . . .	. . . .
. . . .	. . . .
. . . .	. . . .
. . . .	. . . .
. . . .	. . . .
. . . .	. . . .
. . . .	. . . .
. . . .	. . . .
. . . .	. . . .
. . . .	. . . .

Exactly how and when you start tackling your fears is largely up to you. You could face one fear each week of your six-week programme. Alternatively, you could wait until you have completed some of the programme to face your first fear – by then you will have made some progress and will be feeling better about yourself.

If you feel any anxiety or panic as the task approaches, you may benefit from some deep breathing to help you relax. Take three deep breaths in and out and relax. Then, inhale deeply and imagine yourself filling up with brilliant white light. Exhale and imagine yourself breathing out bright red light. Continue breathing in this way until you feel calm and relaxed. If you now feel okay to continue with your challenge, then proceed; if not, wait until you feel more comfortable in yourself. There's no need to face any fear until you are ready.

Keep in mind what actually happens when you face a fear. As you anticipate the coming challenge, you experience very low-vibrational thoughts and feelings ('I'm not good enough', 'What if I fail?'). Then when you succeed, your thoughts and emotions become very high-vibrational ('I did it', 'I succeeded', 'I'm worthy'). This change in your energy field happens very quickly, giving you a wonderful feeling of exhilaration.

You can also use affirmations to help you overcome your fears. For example, if you dread going to work, every day when you get up in the morning repeat ten times, 'I can do this job well.' Repeat it again before you go to bed. (For more on affirmations see pages 105–8.) You can also use visualisation, imagining yourself, for example, going confidently to work, achieving what you set out to do once you are there, and feeling really good about your work environment. (For more on visualisation see pages 109–17)

Eleanor Roosevelt said:

You gain strength, courage and confidence by every experience in which you really stop to look fear in the face ... You must do the thing you think you cannot do.

This exercise is a great way of doing just that – and feeling really great about yourself.

Dealing with setbacks

Everyone following an HVT programme experiences setbacks at times. Very often people do well for several weeks and then begin to come up with excuses for why they should not continue with the programme. In other words, they find a way to talk themselves out of success.

I remember one man who had faced his fears and reached a point where he could smell the success that would improve his life. But as he moved out of his restrictive comfort zone, he became so anxious that he made himself ill. Fortunately, I and the other people on the course were there to support him and talk him through it.

Once he understood what was going on, he found the energy to move forward again, pushing aside the restrictions that were dragging him back.

When your own fears of success surface, face them, using the knowledge that HVT has given you. Tell yourself how great you are – and believe it. Take a deep breath and push your way forward. This in itself is another victory that will make you feel good about yourself.

Burn Your Bridges

Burning your bridges means making a very powerful statement of commitment to change, leaving no way of turning back. You are declaring to your subconscious mind that you are focused on your objective and will not consider the possibility of failure. This is what I did when I made that decision not to give in until I had sold my quota of magazines (see pages 77–8). Commitment has the effect of silencing your subconscious mind, cancelling out its low-vibrational chatter and enabling your frequency to rise accordingly, moving you into a much more productive vibrational zone. When this happens, you function at much closer to your full potential, and you will be amazed at what you can achieve.

Historic proof that it works
There is a famous story about Ulysses. On arriving at Troy he found his army vastly outnumbered by that of the Trojans and ordered that all of his ships should be destroyed. He then declared to his army that they must return home in their enemy's ships or face certain death. Against all the odds, they defeated the Trojans and returned home victorious.

By leaving no way back, Ulysses made a very powerful statement not only to his own army, whose lives now depended on victory, but also to the Trojans. If the Trojan

Ulysses used absolute conviction to gain his objective.

army had any doubts about the conviction of their opponents, these doubts were surely quashed.

Muhammad Ali was a great exponent of burning bridges. He often predicted his own victory in a very public way and sometimes even stated the round in which he would win. This committed him to his objective and cast doubts in the mind of his opponent. Doubts, of course, are negative thoughts that pull down the frequency of the person entertaining them. This impairs their performance, giving an advantage to their opponent.

How you can make this work for you

Whether you are taking your driving test, stopping smoking or going on a diet, tell all your friends what you are doing and that you are going to succeed. You will then be seriously motivated if your willpower begins to weaken. This will help you to override your subconscious mind when it starts to complain – as it surely will, because, as we know, any time you step outside your comfort zone you are declaring war on your subconscious.

It helps to be specific when you are setting yourself targets, but there is more than one way of doing this. For example, you could set yourself the target of finding a new job within six months, or asking your boss for a rise. Alternatively, you could set yourself a negative target, for example declaring that you will never again agree to complete a job that someone else should do when in reality you have less time than the other person.

It takes a lot of strength and courage to burn your bridges, but it is a very effective way of committing yourself and it helps to close the door on self-doubt and the low-vibrational energy that is always ready to creep in and drag down your personal energy frequency.

Leave no avenues of escape and you will galvanise yourself for success.

Don't Open the Door to Doubt

To achieve peak performance in anything, we have to be totally committed and believe 100 per cent that we can do it. Doubt leaves the door open for low-vibrational energy to creep in and pull down our personal energy frequency, which means that we are falling short of our potential. The more intense the low-vibrational thoughts, the further we fall short of our potential.

Will you make that sale? Yes!

Let's say, for example, you are a vacuum cleaner salesman about to knock on somebody's door to try to make a sale. As you approach the door you feel confident, your personal energy field is vibrating at a high frequency, so you are close to achieving your potential, which is to complete the sale. As you get closer to the front door, you catch a glimpse of the open garage door and notice that the car in it is old and a bit rusty. 'They probably don't have much money,' you think, 'or they wouldn't have a car like that.' This opens your mind to doubts, and in floods the low-vibrational energy. Suddenly you feel a little less confident, and you start to entertain thoughts like, 'I hope this isn't going to be a waste of my time' and ' I knew this would happen; just my luck.' By the time the front door is opened, you are in a low-vibrational zone, way below your potential, which means you have probably lost the sale in your own mind before you have even opened your mouth. The man who answers the door isn't interested in buying anything, so off you trudge to the next house, your sense of failure only confirmed.

If this goes on, your potential to make a sale will continue to drop as the low-vibrational energy takes hold. To complete the vicious circle, your customers will be less inclined to buy from you if your personal energy frequency is low, as any interaction with you will pull down their own energy frequency, which will make them want to get you away from their door as soon as possible. People can sense the frequency of your energy field and will respond to it instinctively.

Of course, you may still make the odd sale, and when you do, just imagine how great it feels! Like winning the Lotto, the Premier League or the Superbowl! The good feelings that the sale brings pull up your energy frequency, making the next call easier and a sale more likely.

Now let's look at the same scenario from a different – high-vibrational – perspective. Our high-vibrational salesman catches a glimpse of the same old rusty car, but he's determined not to lose any sales, so he thinks, 'They don't spend much on their car, so they should have enough money to buy a vacuum cleaner.' This way of thinking raises his personal energy frequency slightly, moving him into a higher frequency zone and drawing him nearer to his potential, which is to make a sale. And, in fact, even if he doesn't make this sale, his positive attitude will keep his energy levels up, as he simply will not allow himself to be put off.

I am sure the salespeople out there are familiar with the rollercoaster ride of highs and lows that can make for some tough days at work. But the people who make the best sales are the ones with the fewest doubts about their ability to make a sale, those who don't take the inevitable rejections personally and let themselves be dragged down. Self-belief is the key. If you truly believe something, then you can make it happen.

Make it true for you

This is not only true for people working in sales, of course. The principle applies to all of us: teachers, nurses, office workers, farmers, factory workers, waitresses. If we believe in ourselves and believe we can succeed, then we will give ourselves the greatest possible chance of success. If we hold on to high-vibrational thought patterns and shrug off low-vibrational ones as we go through our day, we will feel better about ourselves, achieve more and feel happier.

Take the waitress who comes to work with a high-vibrational attitude. She'll smile more, the customers will be more responsive and friendly and will almost certainly tip better. If someone spills chicken soup down her skirt, she won't enjoy it much, but she won't let it get her down. Contrast with this the low-vibrational attitude of her colleague, who finds it hard to motivate herself and so is slow in her work, causing the customers to complain (which upsets her and further lowers her vibrational level) and then leave without giving her a tip. You can see how this cycle works against her.

Use high-vibrational energy to attract others to you

We have already noted that when we interact we affect each other's energy levels. This means that you can use your own energy zone to draw people towards you – or repel them.

I was once working with a colleague in a shopping centre, selling magazines to the public. We were having quite a successful day and chatting occasionally as we

High-vibrational energy is attractive to other people, whereas low-vibrational energy repels them.

looked out for customers. For some reason, we started talking about a difficult situation we were experiencing at the office. The more we talked, the more low-vibrational we became. I began to feel angry and worried as the office problem invaded my mind. Then I noticed that people were beginning to give us a wide berth – literally keeping as far away from us as they could – so, of course, we had no hope of a sale.

After about 20 minutes, my colleague made a joke and we began to laugh. Our mood lifted straight away. The next thing I knew, a lady and gentleman approached us to ask what we were selling and promptly bought a magazine. It wasn't long before we had sold all our stock.

If you understand HVT, it's not difficult to recognise what was happening. When my colleague and I were discussing the negative office situation, our combined personal energy fields created a bubble of low-vibrational energy that repelled customers. Once we surrounded ourselves with high-vibrational energy, on the other hand, customers were keen to come over to us.

Quite simply, high-vibrational energy makes us more attractive, and if we feel more attractive, we can't fail to feel great about ourselves.

Taking the Issue to the Comfort Zone

Before we move on to the six-week programme, let's just remind ourselves what we are ultimately trying to achieve, which is to reprogramme your comfort zone so that it works in your favour. Your subconscious mind established a set of rules when you were young to govern what it sees as normal for you, and it is monitoring you so that you stay within these boundaries. If you suffer from low self-esteem, it is because you feel – for whatever reason – that you don't deserve any better.

This may be because you were put down as a child by a member of your family and have grown up to expect this as normal. It may be because you have suffered a traumatic event. The reason for your lack of self-love is not important as we all suffer from this to some degree. What is important is that you understand that it is on this basis that your comfort zone is formed and that to change your life you must change your comfort zone.

The power of the subconscious
Let's look at an extreme example to clarify how this works. We have all heard about, or perhaps know, people whose lives have fallen apart; maybe they are drinking excessively,

are addicted to drugs or are indulging in anti-social behaviour. How have they ended up in this situation?

Even a minor negative event, if it is repeated sufficiently frequently in childhood, may be enough to establish in a person's mind that they are not deserving of any of the good things in life. Once their subconscious accepts this belief, their behaviour is almost guaranteed to make sure they get only the worst. They will tend to avoid work at school, get into the wrong crowd, and accept negative criticism and live up to it. In short, the cycle of low-vibrational energy in their life will spiral downwards – with disastrous consequences.

Once a person is in that cycle, it is very difficult to break out of it. But it is not impossible. With the help of HVT anyone can understand what is happening and put a stop to it permanently.

I once worked with a chap who was very quiet and sensitive. He was hard-working and always did his job well enough, but he never excelled at anything. He was very self-effacing and would often put himself down in conversation. It was almost as if he so fully expected people to make jokes at his expense or run him down that he tried to get in first and do it for them. Promotions were available within the department on more than one occasion, but he never put himself forward for them, and, in fact, his superiors probably did not consider him for them. He was stuck within a comfort zone that was, at best, average, and that was what he saw as his potential. If only he had known about high-vibrational thinking, who knows what he might have achieved?

The subconscious mind is so powerful that what it expects to happen in your life more than likely will. In this case, the guy expected to live a fairly mundane and lacklustre life, and so that is what happened.

You are worth it!

If you recognise yourself in any of the examples in the previous section, you need to start reprogramming your subconscious. Begin by telling yourself you are worth just as much as anyone else – and keep on telling yourself. Write it down, post it on the wall, jot it down in your notebook. Don't miss any opportunity to tell yourself how wonderful you are. There's any number of ways you can do this, but specific statements usually work best, as they will be more believable.

Try some of these ideas. Tell yourself:

▶ I have great hair.
▶ I'm a brilliant cook.
▶ I have a good figure.
▶ I'm great at football.
▶ I presented an excellent report for work.
▶ I'm a kind and caring person.
▶ My bum looks stunning in this!

Keep on at yourself all the time, remarking on every small success. You'll be surprised at how quickly they mount up and how much high-vibrational energy you generate with each compliment.

Take it a step at a time

Once you have affirmed how great you are, you can start tackling specific activities and trying to change your habits. Do this gradually. Don't try to take on everything at once or you will feel overwhelmed. If, for example, you are going out for a drink with friends, spend half an hour before you leave thinking about all the good things that could happen while you are out. You could go to a lively bar – if that's what you like – and chat to some interesting people. You could enjoy a few pints of your favourite beer.

You could feel good in your new shirt. You could have a good time with great friends. Brush away any negative thoughts. Although you probably won't succeed completely the first time you do this exercise, nevertheless it will have a positive impact on your energy levels, and each time you do it, you will find it easier.

Imagine, for example, that you are going for a job interview. Prepare for it by playing through the occasion in your mind. See yourself having a shower, doing your hair and putting on your smartest clothes. You plan your route to the interview venue, make sure you get there on time and walk confidently into the offices. You smile, introduce yourself calmly and clearly to the receptionist, and breathe deeply and think about what you are going to say as you wait. When you meet the interviewer, you offer your hand and smile.

Continue running the interview through your head, seeing yourself giving clear and sensible answers. Remember, if you visualise a smooth and impressive interview enough times, this is exactly what you will deliver. When you go to the actual interview, your energy will be in the high zone, you will feel more confident and you will be far more likely to succeed.

Re-evaluate yourself

Think about the various areas of your life and what you would like in them. Don't go over the top; be realistic. But don't accept negative ideas either. Try to cover all aspects of your life. Once you have a list of about 20 things, type or write it out neatly and pin it somewhere where you can see it every day. Write your goals in the present tense, as if you have already achieved them. Remember, your subconscious delivers to you exactly what you ask for. If you put your target in the future, this is what you will get: something that you are always striving for but never quite achieving.

If you don't want anyone else to see it, keep it under your pillow and look at it night and morning.

Here are a few ideas to get you started:

- ▸ I have a secure job as a mechanic.
- ▸ I have a holiday in the sun every summer.
- ▸ I have attained a promotion.
- ▸ My social circle has increased.

Keep reminding yourself of these successes and telling yourself that you deserved them. They are within your grasp. Eventually, your subconscious will get the message and move the boundaries of your comfort zone to a better and more rewarding position. Remember that belief is the key to success. You only have to convince your subconscious mind that what you want to achieve is a good thing and it will happen.

Three Steps to Feeling Great About Yourself

The final sections of the book focus on the fundamental issue of raising your average vibrational energy level. It is your action plan for changing your life.

This section of the book is geared to enabling you to make the necessary changes to ensure that low-vibrational thinking is eradicated from your life permanently. This means reprogramming your subconscious mind to believe that you are a great person, that you deserve to be happy, successful and loved.

The aim of the exercises in the remainder of the book is to help you become more high-frequency in your general thinking and eliminate any negative thought patterns that you may have been carrying. This will have the effect of increasing your personal energy frequency, which in turn will push the barriers of your comfort zone. There are three steps in this process:

▸ Step 1: accept responsibility for your life.
▸ Step 2: make the commitment to improve your self-image and self-esteem.
▸ Step 3: undertake a six-week programme of practical exercises to reprogramme your subconscious mind.

Step 1: Accepting responsibility

If you are not achieving your potential, if you feel unloved and a failure, it is because at some level of your subconscious mind you believe that this is what you deserve. I believe that most of us feel like this at one time or another, but for you this feeling may have become a major issue that conditions your whole life.

The act of accepting responsibility for what happens in our lives empowers. It gives us the control that we need to be able to do something about our situation. If we don't accept responsibility, we are in effect giving our power away and blaming outside factors for what happens in our lives. It is vital to accept the fact that you are in control and can do something to enable you to move forward in a positive and constructive way.

Step 2: Making the commitment

You must be totally committed to changing your life for the better if you really want to move forward, raise your self-esteem and feel great about yourself. A very strange thing happens when you truly commit yourself – you tap into an extraordinary force that raises your levels of power and control far beyond what you would normally expect.

Step 3: Undertaking the programme

Nothing is achieved without work, but it is not difficult to work through the simple exercises I provide. If you repeat them regularly, they will make a huge difference to your life. In addition to the small steps I have guided you through so far in this section of the book, I will take you through some proven and powerful affirmation and visualisation exercises designed to raise the frequency of your personal energy field on a permanent basis.

Your self-improvement programme

The programme for self-improvement I am setting you is to be followed over a six-week period, which in my experience is the optimum period to initiate change. However, I strongly recommend that you repeat this six-week module four times, with a one-week rest period in between each module. This will take you a total of 27 weeks, which is the six months that I personally found cemented permanent change.

This is what you will have to do:

▸ Make a statement of your acceptance of responsibility and repeat it as often as you like.
▸ Make a commitment to raising your self-esteem and repeat it as often as you like.
▸ Dedicate your commitment to someone special to you.
▸ Read the high-vibrational affirmation you have been provided with for each week and then write six more of your own.
▸ Repeat the week's affirmations ten times in the morning and ten times in the evening every day.
▸ Use two visualisation exercises every day. I have provided the first two; you need to develop ten more of your own.

All this should take you ten or fifteen minutes a day – not much when the results will change your life!

Use the timetable on pages 117–24 to monitor your progress, ticking off the exercises as you do them. This will help you to stay focused and bring an element of discipline to your programme.

Accepting Responsibility

Taking responsibility is vital to raising your self-esteem and feeling good about yourself. This may involve forgiving others who you feel are responsible for your current position. Once you have accepted responsibility for what is happening in your life, you will have the control to do something about it.

The act of acceptance will also make you aware of a whole host of low-vibrational thought patterns. These flourish in a mind that gives its power away. 'Poor me', 'Why am I so unlucky?', 'Everybody is against me', 'It's not my fault' – we are all guilty of these kinds of thoughts, but it is essential to try to avoid them. They are low-vibrational and serve only one purpose: that is, to drag down your energy frequency, making life much harder for you. You are much more likely to stay stuck in a low-vibrational state if you blame other people for your plight. So, as you can see, step one is vitally important. You cannot move forward until you have acknowledged that you are responsible for your life.

Your acceptance statement

Think carefully about your decision to accept that you are responsible for your life and put it in writing. This will strengthen your belief. You can either copy the following acceptance statement, filling in the date and your name, or write your own.

From today, the .... of .... 20...,
I, ..., accept full responsibility for my
life. I realise that there is no point in holding on to any low-
vibrational feelings and emotions from the past. I release any
negative energy that I am holding on to. From this moment I
accept total responsibility.

You must take total responsibility for your new life in order
to succeed.

Strengthen yourself every day

Repeat your acceptance over to yourself several times. As you do so, see yourself letting go of all your low-vibrational energy and allowing your energy frequency to rise as you move your life forward into a new and exciting future.

Read through your acceptance statement every morning, as many times as you like, and any time you feel your old low-vibrational feelings creeping back.

Making the Commitment

Being totally committed to raising your energy vibration will give you extraordinary power. The dramatist Goethe wrote:

The moment one commits oneself, then providence moves too. All sorts of things occur to help one that would never have otherwise occurred. A whole new stream of events, all manner of unforeseen incidents and chance meetings, and material assistance come forth which no one could have dreamt would appear.

Something quite magical occurs when we make a committed decision. When our intention is totally focused, we tap into the incredible power of the subconscious mind and enlist its full support in our chosen endeavour. Normally, the subconscious mind sticks to its comfort zone, placing restrictions on our intentions and achievements. However, when our commitment is total, we seem to be able to override subconscious programming and access its incredible potential. If you commit completely, then the possibility of failure is not even a consideration.

What real commitment can achieve

I remember a story a policeman told me about a car accident he attended one night. A young child was trapped under one of the cars, and four burly policemen were

attempting to lift the car off the child. They struggled
without success; the car was just too heavy to move. Then
the mother of the child took hold of the car and lifted it off
the child by herself. The policemen looked on in amazement
at what seemed impossible. What had happened was that
the woman had totally committed herself to lifting the car,
and her focused commitment had overridden her
programming about what was and wasn't possible.

The act of commitment overrides limitations created by our belief system, by society and by our upbringing, and enables us to reach our true potential. Once Roger Bannister had broken the four-minute mile and proved that what had been seen as impossible was, in fact, possible, four or five other athletes also achieved the four-minute mile within weeks.

The deeper your commitment, the fewer problems your subconscious programming will cause you. You must leave no exit strategies, allow no 'maybes' or attitudes of 'we will see how it goes'. This is a sure-fire way of guaranteeing failure. You must focus on success – nothing else will do.

Your commitment

You will find that six weeks is a comfortable time period in which to stay focused on your goal, determined and in control without too much interference from your subconscious mind.

Think carefully about your commitment to what you want to achieve. Then either copy the following commitment statement, filling in the date and your name, or write your own.

From today, the .... of .... 20...,
I, ..., commit to focus on my goal with all my strength for the next six weeks. I will succeed in my desire to carry out the exercises and disciplines required, and I will not fail.

Now read your commitment statement out loud as many times as you like. Any time you feel your willpower beginning to weaken, refer back to your dedication to reinforce your commitment.

Dedicate your commitment

A good way to reinforce your commitment is to dedicate your goal to somebody special to you, perhaps your son or daughter, your mother or father, or your partner. It also helps if you can put the dedication in writing, so that you can refer back to it in moments of weakness. Write down the name of the person and why you are choosing them for your dedication. This may simply be because you love them, or it may be because you want to be able to be more supportive towards them or because you respect them and want to be more like them.

I, ..., dedicate the following six weeks to .... because ....
..
I will make you very proud of me.

This act of dedication will help to sustain you when your subconscious starts complaining and your determination and willpower weaken.

Making progress

It took me six months to make real permanent changes within my life, although this may not necessarily be the case for you. However, it will take some time, and that means plenty of opportunities for your subconscious mind to find ways to sabotage your efforts. Watch out for thoughts that are counterproductive to your goal. My subconscious went very quiet for a couple of weeks when faced with failure; then, when I had become complacent in my focus, it suddenly reappeared and was back to its old tricks!

You will know you are really beginning to succeed when quite suddenly you find that the effort you have had to summon up on a daily basis to push towards your desired goal lessens and perhaps even disappears.

Think what it is like when you first join a gym. Your initial enthusiasm propels you through the first few visits. Then your subconscious starts to get bored and begins to find reasons for you to stay at home. If you persist and become healthier, it no longer recognises the new you as fitting within its comfort zone and tries to keep you at the lower frequency level where it feels you belong. But if you keep going nevertheless, one day you will suddenly realise that you just can't face life without going to the gym. In fact, if you don't go, you will probably feel down and lethargic. This is your new comfort zone – and this one is good for you!

This process is one that we go through whenever we wish to make positive changes in our life. The trick is to understand what is going on in your own mind. This will enable you to stay committed to your goal and in control of your subconscious mind. You must show it who is boss.

Your Affirmations

I recommend two main methods for helping you raise your energy vibration: affirmation and visualisation. Both are really simple and so are easy to put into practice. They rely for their power on repetition, and – believe me – they are a powerful way to change your life.

A high–vibrational energy field vibrates faster and expands much further than a low–vibrational energy field.

The advantage of these techniques is that they can be done in small corners of your day and don't need to impact detrimentally on your routine. If you want to, you can do them quietly on your own and no-one else need be involved. This can be a real help in building up your personal strength and raising your vibrational energy levels in order to help you take action to feel great about yourself.

Positive affirmations

Affirmations are powerful statements that you repeat to yourself so often that you persuade your subconscious mind to accept them as being true. If you continually bombard yourself with these statements, you will reprogramme your subconscious mind, thus redefining the boundaries of your comfort zone. Obviously, you need to use powerful high-vibrational statements, which you can tailor to your own particular needs. This will have the effect of replacing low-vibrational thought patterns with high-vibrational thought patterns and raising the frequency of your personal energy field. The longer you keep this up, the more permanent the rise in frequency will be.

As we have already seen, your life will run a lot more smoothly at the higher frequency levels, so it makes sense to pursue with vigour any methods you have at your disposal to achieve a higher vibrational level.

Writing your affirmations

Here are some examples of affirmations you might use. You can choose anything that strengthens your purpose and brings positive energy into your life.

- ▸ I love and approve of myself.
- ▸ I attract success and wealth into my life.
- ▸ I radiate powerful positive energy.
- ▸ I feel great every day.

- ▶ I am powerful and strong.
- ▶ I am positive.
- ▶ I am in control of my life.
- ▶ I have absolute respect for myself.
- ▶ I am a wonderful person.

Affirmations should be written in the present tense, as if you have already attained them. They should not admit of any doubts.

You could write your affirmations on flash cards and keep them in your purse or wallet. Or stick them somewhere where you will see them as you go about your day, for example on the fridge.

Using your affirmations

Each week you will read, preferably out loud, six high-vibrational affirmations. Read them ten times every morning and ten times every night, just before you go to sleep. Use the same affirmations for the course of a week, then move on to the next set of six. Keep repeating your favourite affirmations to yourself all day long, whenever you can find the time. After a couple of weeks you will be amazed at how different you feel.

Sometimes, after three to four weeks, you may feel that the affirmations are not really working any more. Don't let this deter you. This is a crucial point, at which you must keep up the bombardment of high-vibrational energy. Your subconscious mind can be very clever and will use all of its persuasive powers to convince you to desist. Do not give in. Keep going. The boundaries of your comfort zone are changing without you realising it. After six weeks you will have made noticeable progress.

At the end of the first six-week period, you may want to change some of your affirmations before you begin your next six-week course.

If you really believe it, you'll be on the way to achieving it.

Believe me, you can't bombard your subconscious mind enough! You should live and breathe high-vibrational thoughts. They will push up the frequency of your personal energy field, changing your life for the better in the process. The more high-vibrational thoughts you think, the more used to them your mind will become. You are drowning out low-vibrational thoughts, not allowing them to take hold and drag down your personal energy frequency. If you do this enough, your subconscious mind will accept that this higher frequency state is the norm for you, and then this will become your natural state of being.

Your Visualisations

Walt Disney said, 'If you can dream it, you can do it.' That's what visualisation is all about.

Visualisation is a powerful tool, which you can use to help reprogramme your subconscious mind. What you are doing is convincing your subconscious mind that you are capable of achieving the subject of your visualisation. The secret to success in any area of life is to believe that you can do it, or – to be more precise – to make your subconscious mind believe that you can do it. As the real source of your unlimited potential is within your subconscious mind, this is where your true capabilities lie.

Visualisation can help you to mould your expectations to your advantage.

Belief is the key to success, as to truly believe eliminates any doubts from your mind and moves you into a frequency zone where anything is possible. This is the zone where you are calm, happy, and detached from the outcome of your objective (becoming over-involved could open the door to doubt and pull your frequency level down into a less productive zone). The secret is to relax, know that you will succeed and trust in your ability; just enjoy the moment and bask in the high vibrations. Then, almost without thinking about your objective, allow everything to flow naturally. Success will be almost guaranteed.

How to visualise

A visualisation is nothing more complicated than a high-powered daydream! You simply need to make yourself comfortable, relax and give yourself completely to your imagination. Learn to see yourself in positive situations in which you achieve success in everything that you do. Imagine yourself as the person you want to be. Feel the emotions you will feel when you become this person. Remember, you have only to believe in something to make it a reality.

The key to successful visualisation is your imagination: learn to use it to your advantage. See yourself in successful situations, whether they relate to work, relationships or leisure. The more you use visualisation, the better you will become at it and the easier it will be for your subconscious to accept the visualisation as real. Truly believing something will make it happen.

Your visualisation programme

For this programme, you should do two visualisation exercises every day for the six-week period. The best times are when you wake up in the morning, as this will set your energy levels on high vibration for the remainder of the day, and last thing at night, to dispel any low-vibrational thoughts that have crept in during your day. Each visualisation takes about five minutes.

I have provided two visualisations. Use these for the first two weeks and then create two more yourself for each following week. Visualisation is much more effective if you incorporate things that are personal to you. Include anything that makes you feel good about yourself. Make time in your timetable to plan and write your visualisation exercises.

Comfort your inner child visualisation

Your life is merely a reflection of what your subconscious mind believes you deserve. As we have already noted, our subconscious mind is also known as our inner child, because it has all the attributes and characteristics of a small child. As you know, it has an established comfort zone, which is the way it is programmed to think life should be for you and where it wants you to remain. Whether this is good or bad for you is irrelevant, as your inner child cannot differentiate between the two.

Comforting your inner child is beneficial to many areas of your life. It allows you to acknowledge the importance of your subconscious while at the same time letting go of any low-vibrational thought patterns that may have taken root there, perhaps some time ago. When looking to move your life forward, it is important to clear out these low-frequency feelings and emotions, otherwise they will hold you back and hamper your progress as if you were carrying a dead weight.

There are many reasons why you may need to give your inner child some attention, for example because you have undergone a divorce, lost a job or been badly treated in some way. It is vital to comfort your inner child if you are grieving for a loved one. The grieving process always takes time. However, working with the inner child can

Comforting your inner child shows them that you love them;
when your inner child feels loved, they will be much more
helpful to you as you negotiate life's hurdles.

make the healing process smoother. If we spend all our
time giving attention to our adult self (conscious mind) but
ignore our inner child (subconscious mind) the pain will
never ease. You need to take time to explain to your inner
child what has happened, and visualisation is a great way
to do this.

When my father died, I was a mature adult of 37 years
and, after the initial grief, I expected to cope well and soon
be able to get on with my life. A few months after the
death, however, I began to notice that I had become
withdrawn and non-communicative, not joining in
conversations. I was depressed and felt that I was losing
confidence, which made me quite concerned.

I decided to seek help. I read a number of books on
coping with the death of a parent, but none offered me the
support I needed. I attended a one-day bereavement

workshop and immediately afterwards felt a slight lift in my mood, but within hours I had fallen back into my depression. It was chancing on a chapter in a psychology book about the inner child that helped me to understand what was going on. I had been giving all my attention to my conscious mind, leaving my inner child grieving without support. This kept me in a low-frequency zone of sadness and depression. I immediately began to do a visualisation exercise to comfort my inner child. I explained to him that I loved him very much and that I would take care of him now. I brought my dad into the exercise to reassure him that he was going to be okay. To my amazement, several months of depression were alleviated in ten minutes. I felt as though a huge weight had been lifted from me. It was an astonishing experience, and the result is that I now know how important it is to comfort your inner child.

You can adapt the visualisation in any way you like to make it more personal to you. The stages are as follows:

▸ Read through the visualisation first so you understand what it is trying to achieve and what you need to do.
▸ Get yourself comfortable in a warm room, in a comfortable chair or on your bed.
▸ Close your eyes and relax.
▸ Slowly run through the visualisation in your mind.
▸ Once you have completed the visualisation, lie and relax until you are ready to return to the real world again.

The visualisation

It's a beautiful sunny day. You are gazing out of the bedroom window across green fields. In one of the fields you can see horses running playfully, enjoying the warm sunshine. The horses display such vitality as they run that it fills you with joy just watching them.

You decide to go out for a walk and set off down the stairs to the back door. As you reach the bottom of the stairs you see a small child sitting on the floor playing with some toys. It is you at five years old: your inner child. 'Come on, let's go for a walk,' you say. Your inner child smiles from ear to ear as they jump up and take hold of your hand.

When you walk outside, the warmth of the sun hits you and you feel happy and alive. Your inner child runs off giggling, overcome with joy. You chase after them, and they try to run away from you, laughing and screaming. You sweep them up into your arms, giving them a big hug and kiss on the cheek. 'I love you,' you say, as you hold them close, feeling the warmth of the love between you.

The birdsong seems louder than ever today. The horses see you near the fence and come trotting over. 'Watch me feed the horses,' you say to your inner child, pulling up a handful of grass. As the horses gently munch on the grass, your inner child looks on in amazement. 'Stroke the horse,' you say, gently taking your inner child's hand and rubbing it on the horse's head. You are both so happy together. You explain to your inner child that you love them very much and you will always be there to love and take care of them.

You tell your inner child that you are going to do a six-week programme that will make life much better for you both. It will help you get a better job and have a happier life. Explain that this also means you will be able to buy a new wide-screen television and go on more holidays. See your inner child happy at your announcement and excited about the future. Set off back to the house, both you and the child very happy and content with life.

Success visualisation exercise

This visualisation exercise is, again, intended to help you get in touch with your inner child and make you feel good. Remember, you can adapt it in whatever way you like to suit you. The aim is to get in touch with your subconscious and feel good about yourself. For example, you can use it to see yourself dealing successfully with everyday events such as presenting a report, seeing the boss about a problem, or even facing a critical colleague who says you can't even make a decent cup of tea. It really doesn't matter what it is as long as it's right for you. Repeat the visualisation as often as you like. Remember, you are capable of whatever you believe you are, and visualisation is a very useful tool in enlisting the support of your immensely powerful subconscious mind. Remember to spend a few minutes relaxing and coming slowly back to the real world after you have finished your visualisation.

The visualisation

It's a gorgeous day as you set off to work, and you feel on top of the world, full of confidence about the important exam you are taking today. When you get to the bus stop, you notice your inner child beside you, and you jump on the bus together. You dig into your pocket for the fare, and the two of you sit down to enjoy the bus ride together.

'We will do well today. I feel really good about this exam,' you tell your inner child. Your inner child looks up at you, rather bemused that you could get excited at the thought of boring exams. 'I'll get us a new computer game and DVD if you help me with this exam,' you tell your inner child. That's hit the button. You see your inner child's eyes light up at the prospect. 'Don't forget that when I pass this exam, we will have a better job, and life will be happier for us, so I want you to help me as much as you can.'

You put your arm around your inner child, hug them and kiss the top of their head. 'I love you very much,' you whisper into their ear.

You soon arrive at the office and seat yourself in the exam room, then get down to work. You work well and feel confident, and before you know it, the exam is over and you and your inner child are dashing off to the ice cream parlour for a treat. You are both so happy.

Once the ice creams are finished, you keep your promise and take your inner child to buy the computer game and DVD. Your inner child is delighted, and this makes you feel good inside.

Soon you are both home, settling down for a cosy night in front of the television, feeling very content with your day.

Visualisation in daily life

Now that you have made contact with your inner child, you may find it beneficial to keep up the relationship. Visualisation is a wonderful way of doing this. You can use it whenever you have a few spare moments in your day. You can also use visualisation in other areas of your life. For example, you may want to use it to help with your job. Set aside five minutes each day to visualise how you want your work day to go; put negative thoughts out of your mind and imagine the best scenario. You may want to use visualisation to improve your relationships. Use your imagination to play out any scene that you feel will help. For example, see yourself and your partner in happy, loving situations. Remember, you just have to truly believe it and it will happen.

Practice is the key to success here. The more often you visualise, the more readily your subconscious mind will accept your visualisations. This will enable you to run through any visualisations that you feel may be appropriate whenever you need them, as practice will have honed your skills, making your subconscious mind open to your suggestions. Visualisation puts you in the driving seat, enabling you to control your subconscious mind rather than it controlling you.

As you use HVT in your life, you will become increasingly aware of the constant tussle taking place between your conscious and your subconscious mind. When you notice this taking place, it may help to spend a little time explaining to your subconscious mind what it is that you are trying to achieve. Make your inner child part of your life and remember that your life will be a lot easier if you can enlist their support in your endeavours. Explain to them the benefits to both of you of what you are doing. Don't forget that they are a child and make it attractive to them. For example, if you are a student taking exams and feeling unsure of your capabilities, ask your inner child to help you. Explain that if you pass your exams, you will be able to get a better, higher-paid job, which means more treats, such as a trip to the zoo or a new computer game. Remember, you are trying to motivate a five-year-old child, so think in terms of what they would like.

Learning to communicate with your inner child is important if you are really to move forward and fully realise your amazing potential. After all, it is the thought patterns that are programmed into the mind of your inner child that dominate your life. In order to make changes in this area it is vital first of all to open the channels of communication.

Your Progress to Feeling Great About Yourself

Use these pages to write your own affirmations, make notes on your personal visualisations and tick off when you have completed your tasks. It will help to keep you on track, give you focus and purpose, and also reassure you that things are improving all the time.

My acceptance statement

. . . .
. . . .
. . . .
. . . .

My commitment statement

. . . .
. . . .
. . . .
. . . .

My dedication

. . . .
. . . .
. . . .
. . . .

Week 1
My affirmations

▸ I love and approve of myself.

▸ . . . .

▸ . . . .

▸ . . . .

▸ . . . .

▸ . . . .

My visualisations

▸ Comfort your inner child visualisation (see pages 111–4).

▸ Success visualisation (see pages 114–6).

My checklist

Day	Morning affirmations	Morning visualisation	Evening affirmations	Evening visualisation
Monday				
Tuesday				
Wednesday				
Thursday				
Friday				
Saturday				
Sunday				

Week 2
My affirmations

▶   I feel great every day.

▶   . . . .

▶   . . . .

▶   . . . .

▶   . . . .

▶   . . . .

My visualisations

▶   . . . .

▶   . . . .

My checklist

Day	Morning affirmations	Morning visualisation	Evening affirmations	Evening visualisation
Monday				
Tuesday				
Wednesday				
Thursday				
Friday				
Saturday				
Sunday				

Week 3
My affirmations

▶ I have absolute respect for myself.

▶ ....

▶ ....

▶ ....

▶ ....

▶ ....

My visualisations

▶ ....

▶ ....

My checklist

Day	Morning affirmations	Morning visualisation	Evening affirmations	Evening visualisation
Monday				
Tuesday				
Wednesday				
Thursday				
Friday				
Saturday				
Sunday				

Week 4
My affirmations

▶ I am powerful and strong.

▶ . . . .

▶ . . . .

▶ . . . .

▶ . . . .

▶ . . . .

My visualisations

▶ . . . .

▶ . . . .

My checklist

Day	Morning affirmations	Morning visualisation	Evening affirmations	Evening visualisation
Monday				
Tuesday				
Wednesday				
Thursday				
Friday				
Saturday				
Sunday				

Week 5
My affirmations

▶ I radiate powerful positive energy.

▶ ....

▶ ....

▶ ....

▶ ....

▶ ....

My visualisations

▶ ....

▶ ....

My checklist

Day	Morning affirmations	Morning visualisation	Evening affirmations	Evening visualisation
Monday				
Tuesday				
Wednesday				
Thursday				
Friday				
Saturday				
Sunday				

Week 6
My affirmations

▶ I am a wonderful person.

▶ . . . .

▶ . . . .

▶ . . . .

▶ . . . .

▶ . . . .

My visualisations

▶ . . . .

▶ . . . .

My checklist

Day	Morning affirmations	Morning visualisation	Evening affirmations	Evening visualisation
Monday				
Tuesday				
Wednesday				
Thursday				
Friday				
Saturday				
Sunday				

Index